KAREN MARTINI started her cooking career at the age of sixteen. She launched the critically acclaimed Melbourne Wine Room, which she ran for fifteen years; was Executive and Founding Chef at Sydney's Icebergs Dining Room and Bar; and in 2004 opened much-loved St Kilda pizzeria, mr. wolf, with her partner, Michael Sapountsis. She has a huge following through her weekly recipe pages in Fairfax's Good Food/Epicure liftouts, her role as a judge on the television series *My Kitchen Rules*, and her long-running spot as resident chef on Channel 7's *Better Homes and Gardens*. Karen is in demand at food festivals around the country and is the author of seven top-selling cookbooks. She lives in Melbourne with Michael and their children, Stella and Amber, and naughty dog Rudi.

karenmartini.com
facebook.com/karen.martini.australia
instagram.com/karen_martini
twitter.com/karen_martini

For Mike, Stella
and Amber

NEW KITCHEN

KAREN MARTINI

plum.

Pan Macmillan Australia

CONTENTS

INTRODUCTION

If I look back at what my pantry would have consisted of fifteen years ago, it would be very different to what it contains today.

Yes, it would still have been packed with spices, good pasta, real balsamic and great extra-virgin olive oil. But now the range of spices has grown substantially, and the array of bottles, jars and packets has become very international. I now always have several types of rice, plenty of whole grains, seeds and nuts, and dried goods that range through Kashmiri chillies, kombu and shiitake. You wouldn't have found gochugaru in my old larder, but it gets used and replaced quite regularly now. Ramen and rice stick noodles jostle with the pasta, and my salt collection has exploded into an obsession.

And it doesn't just include purchased staples, typically there's homemade dukkah, toasted muesli, various breads and a motley collection of repurposed jars full of jams, sauces and all sorts of pickles. My fridge might contain homemade butter and ricotta sitting next to a couple of types of miso and a jar of kimchi. The freezer might be loaded with stock or a deep bone broth, a leftover batch of bao, or even some decadent jamon croquetas, ready for that unexpected party.

And this little tour, more or less, describes how I cook today.

When I was training as a chef, I was immersed in classical technique, learning my trade by cooking the most familiar dishes of traditional French cuisine. As I branched out, my food had an Italian heart, but I always nibbled at other bits of the European Mediterranean, taking in North Africa and dabbling in the Middle East. Over time, China and Southeast Asia have also gripped me pretty firmly, particularly Thailand, and, of late, Japan and Korea have been big inspirations. All of these influences make up the cook I am today: eclectic, not slavishly authentic, but always respectful and constantly interested in experimenting.

And this, to a greater or lesser degree, is true for many of us. Fifteen years ago, the way most of us cooked and ate was very different to the way we cook and eat today.

We are no less in love with the dishes that we grew up with, the food of our childhood homes and the cuisines from our favourite family restaurants, be they Chinese, Italian, Indian, Japanese or Greek. But today, the home-cooked staples of childhood have been remastered, and our demands on those old-school restaurants are very different. Rather than dishes softened to fit an Australian palate, we now crave the more authentic, and seek out food that challenges and excites us.

No longer do we consider China to have one cuisine, but appreciate the distinctions between, say, Cantonese and Sichuan cooking. We recognise the differences between the cooking of northern Italy and the sun-drenched south, between dishes typical of Goa to those of Kashmir. And our affection for the food of the Middle East and the Levant has only grown stronger, with brilliant champions such as Yotam Ottolenghi and Greg Malouf showing us both the history and the amazing possibilities.

Our appreciation of Mexican food has exploded from the caricature of nachos and packet tacos to encompass the deep sophistication of one of the world's great cuisines. Korean food, almost certainly buoyed by the international reach of the game-changing David Chang, has captured our imagination of late, whether with traditional or reimagined fare. The food of the United States has also had a big influence on our palates. From the rise of 'dude food' and reworked American classics to the deeply thoughtful farm-to-table movement inspired by the work of progressive farmers like Joel Salatin.

Eating for good health has never been so exciting, shedding its old boring tag in quite spectacular fashion. There really is nothing more delicious than a wholefoods diet, and it is at the heart of

good cooking – basically the celebration of beautiful produce. So connected to this interest in healthy food, both for wellbeing and as a culinary expression, is a back-to-basics movement, which embraces making everything from scratch: pickling, fermenting, brining, preserving and curing, as well as returning to traditional practices to prepare whole grains, seeds and nuts.

And food isn't just about the cooking. The provenance of our produce has become an important focus for many people. We seek out produce that is grown or reared responsibly, and often locally, produce that has been treated ethically for the benefit of our health, and the welfare of the animals and the land.

All of these influences, amongst many others, have helped to shape the way we shop, cook and eat today. Australian home cooks are so much more worldly, interested and adventurous than they were fifteen years ago. Busy lives may starve us of time, but the interest I see from cooks who want to experiment with new dishes and ingredients and push themselves to learn is phenomenal. This book is a glimpse into the way I cook today, a culmination of influence and experience, both local and international, and a take on so many of these modern culinary influences seen through my filter.

This book detours a little from the traditional narrative. There's a chapter dedicated to reinventing my past, and another to cutlery-free food. And there are a few sweets hiding in the chapters, so, if that's your thing, don't just turn to the back of the book. There are plenty of simple and nourishing dishes as well as exotic and complex feasts, and a big chapter with weekend projects to stock your fridge and pantry and make the week's cooking a (delicious) breeze. I have also included notes, dotted throughout the pages, on some favourite ingredients, or just ones that might be a little unfamiliar, as well as a few personal anecdotes, reflections and ideas.

Cook, eat and enjoy.

HOUSEMADE PANTRY

PROJECTS FOR THE WEEKEND

———

MAKE YOUR OWN BUTTER

SIMPLE ROASTED RASPBERRY JAM

FIG & GINGER JAM

**TOASTED GLUTEN-FREE MUESLI WITH
ALMONDS & BLUEBERRIES**

DATE, SESAME, CHIA, BEETROOT & CACAO POWER BALLS

ACTIVATED WALNUTS WITH SEA SALT & VINEGAR

**SPICED SALTS:
SICHUAN & MANDARIN SALT
CELERY & BLACK PEPPER SALT
CORIANDER & BLACK PEPPER SALT**

DUKKAH

FRESH RICOTTA

MASTER MAYONNAISE

RED ONION & SHERRY JAM

SPICED BLOOD PLUM SAUCE

WATERMELON RIND PICKLE

GOCHUJANG CHILLI SAUCE

SMOKY CHIPOTLE ADOBO

SPICED CHINESE PICKLES

QUICK KIMCHI

**CITRUS-CURED OCEAN TROUT WITH SICHUAN
PEPPER, MANDARIN & SESAME**

CHICKEN BONE BROTH

———

*Making bread for your guests shows a bit of commitment, making your own butter verges on showing off. But don't let that stop you. If you start off with some great dairy you'll end up with beautiful, creamy butter, and it's simply a perfect way to start a dinner, just add some freshly baked bread (the stuff you made earlier) and a little bowl of quality salt flakes. Once you've gone to the trouble, make sure the butter really shines: toss it with boiled new potatoes and soft herbs; finish a risotto with a generous slab; or just melt it into a piece of toasted sourdough. If you want to dress it up further, shave in a little fresh truffle or fold in some garlic, herbs or toasted spices. And don't throw out that buttermilk, it refrigerates well and can be used in baking, or add it to a brine for poultry or pork (try my **Fried Brined Chicken with Corn Slaw** on page 229).*

MAKE YOUR OWN BUTTER

500 g crème fraîche
500 ml cream (35% fat)
500 ml ice-cold water
2 teaspoons salt flakes

Add the crème fraîche and cream to a blender or food processor and process for about 10 minutes, stopping to scrape down the side every now and then. The mix will thicken and then split, with the buttermilk separating from the solids. Drain off the buttermilk and add the iced water. Blitz for 2 minutes. Tip the butter into a strainer to drain off the excess liquid.

Tip the butter out on a clean wooden board and fold and pat back over itself with a spatula or paddle to extract all the liquid. Once it becomes a pale, solid mass, fold in the salt and form into your desired shape. Wrap in waxed paper or place in a container, cover and refrigerate.

MAKES 400–500 G

*This is such a simple method that it almost feels like cheating, but the results speak for themselves – it just might taste even better than a traditionally made jam. You could make this a little more exotic by adding some rose geranium leaves when you add the lemon juice. This is perfect for layering a **Tiered Sponge Cake** (page 214), or just spread it on some sourdough toast or a slice of **Super Seed Loaf** (page 94) with plenty of **Butter**, homemade (page 12) if you're up for it.*

SIMPLE ROASTED RASPBERRY JAM

1.2 kg frozen raspberries
900 g caster sugar
juice of 1 lemon

You will need enough sterilised jars and lids (see page 17) for 4–5 cups of raspberry jam.

Preheat the oven to 170°C fan-forced (190°C conventional).

Add the raspberries to a large ceramic dish and add the sugar to another. Roast both for 40 minutes.

Remove the dishes from the oven and tip the berries into the sugar – the mix will turn to hot lava, so be careful. Stir through the lemon juice and return to the oven for 10 minutes.

Remove from the oven and stir through. Pour the hot jam into the hot jars right to the top – the jam will shrink as it cools. Once cold, seal the jars and store for up to 6 months. Refrigerate after opening.

MAKES 4–5 CUPS

This simple jam is one of my absolute favourites, vying with cherry jam for my affections. This is a pretty handy recipe if you're lucky enough to have a laden fig tree. Alternatively, when in season locally, select the heaviest and ripest figs you can find at the market. Buy figs for jam towards the end of the season – they'll typically be nice and ripe and they just might be more of a bargain.

FIG & GINGER JAM

1 kg ripe figs, stems removed and cut into 1.5-cm slices
800 g caster sugar
100 g ginger, very finely sliced
juice of 2 lemons

You will need enough sterilised jars and lids (see page 17) for 4 cups of fig jam.

Off the heat, add the figs and 100 ml of water to a wide, heavy-based saucepan. Add the sugar and ginger and stir through with your hands to roughly combine. Place the pan over medium heat and bring to a simmer, skimming off any foam or impurities as they appear. Cook, uncovered, for 20 minutes, stirring occasionally but very gently to avoid breaking up the figs. Add the lemon juice and cook for about 10 minutes until a teaspoon of the jam gels on a chilled plate. If you have a candy thermometer, the jam is ready when the temperature reaches 105–106°C.

Once at gelling stage, pour the hot jam into the warm jars right to the top – the jam will shrink as it cools. Once cold, seal the jars and store for up to 6 months. Refrigerate after opening.

MAKES ABOUT 4 CUPS

STERILISING JARS

You can sterilise jars the old-fashioned way by washing, boiling and then drying them in the oven, but for most domestic applications it just isn't necessary. Sure, if you wanted to start preserving fruit, it's better to look into the process in more detail, but for high-sugar jams and preserves, the dishwasher will do the trick. Wash the jars and lids in hot, soapy water and then run through a hot rinse cycle. You can then dry them quickly upturned on a clean tea towel or pop them in a low oven until needed – it's always best for the jars to be warm when adding the preserve. For jams, you can just let them cool before lidding, but if you want a better seal on sauces and chutneys, fill the hot jars with the hot preserve, seal and then flip the jars onto their lids to cool. This will create a vacuum seal and the lids will depress in the middle. While this is a better seal, its strength is not always consistent and it is not as reliable as traditional processing for long-term preserving.

This lightly toasted muesli has a subtle hint of warm spice and a fresh lilt of orange zest, perfect with some fresh or poached fruit, a dollop of thick and creamy yoghurt and a drizzle of fragrant honey. A handful also makes a great snack, so pack a small bag for school or work.

TOASTED GLUTEN-FREE MUESLI WITH ALMONDS & BLUEBERRIES

200 g golden syrup
80 ml coconut oil
1 whole nutmeg, finely grated
2 teaspoons ground cinnamon
finely grated zest of 1 orange
150 g (1 cup) raw almonds
80 g (1 cup) flaked almonds
180 g (1½ cups) sesame seeds
120 g (1 cup) sunflower seeds
130 g (1 cup) pumpkin seeds
30 g (⅓ cup) chia seeds
50 g (3 cups) rice puffs
50 g (2 cups) millet puffs
100 g (1 cup) shredded coconut
1 teaspoon salt flakes
100 g (½ cup) dried blueberries
50 g (¼ cup) sultanas

Preheat the oven to 160°C fan-forced (180°C conventional). Line two baking trays with baking paper.

Add the golden syrup, oil, nutmeg, cinnamon and orange zest to a small saucepan and stir over low–medium heat until loosened and combined.

Add the remaining ingredients except the blueberries and sultanas to a large bowl. Pour over the golden syrup mix and rub through the dry ingredients with your hands until evenly coated.

Spread the mix out evenly on the prepared trays and bake for 10 minutes, stirring after 5 minutes to toast evenly. Set aside to cool on the trays before mixing through the blueberries and sultanas. Store in an airtight container.

MAKES ABOUT 1 KG

I've played with a few different combinations for these deliciously healthy treats, but this is easily my favourite. There's good natural sweetness from the dates and honey, but it's balanced with the savoury seeds and bitterness of the cacao nibs. You could omit the beetroot powder, if you like, but it adds a lovely, earthy sweetness and the colour is amazing.

DATE, SESAME, CHIA, BEETROOT & CACAO POWER BALLS

200 g sesame seeds
100 g honey
2½ tablespoons coconut oil
2 tablespoons raw cacao powder
1 heaped teaspoon ground ginger
1 heaped teaspoon ground cinnamon
100 g beetroot powder
100 g pumpkin seeds
50 g almond meal
30 g chia seeds
200 g fleshy dates, pitted
2 tablespoons tahini
2 teaspoons salt flakes
50 g cacao nibs

Toast the sesame seeds lightly in a dry frying pan over medium heat until lightly coloured and starting to crackle. Set aside to cool.

Add the honey, oil, cacao powder, spices and 3 tablespoons of the beetroot powder to a small saucepan and gently warm through until melted and combined.

Add the sesame seeds and pumpkin seeds to a food processor and process until a coarse powder. Add the almond meal, chia seeds, dates, tahini and salt and pulse until a coarse mix forms. Add the honey mix and blend to form a smooth paste. Chill for 20 minutes to firm up.

Form the mixture into 30–35 g balls. Roll the balls in the remaining beetroot powder and then gently flatten into the cacao nibs. Store in an airtight container for a couple of days, or refrigerate for up to 10 days.

MAKES 20–30

I don't think walnuts quite get the appreciation they deserve. A fresh local walnut really is a thing of beauty, but so often it's the floury, stale (and often imported) supermarket nuts that form people's impressions. Walnuts are quite fragile once shelled and should be refrigerated to stop the oils becoming rancid. Ideally, buy new season nuts and shell them as required. A big bowl of Victorian walnuts and a good nutcracker are features of my kitchen bench throughout autumn and winter – the squirrels in my house don't need any more encouragement than that. To elevate their many health benefits 'activate' (see below right) the nuts in salted water and then dry gently in the oven. For me, an extra sprinkling of good sea salt flakes and a splash of vinegar takes them to a new level.

ACTIVATED WALNUTS WITH SEA SALT & VINEGAR

500 g walnuts
1 tablespoon sea salt flakes
100 ml malt vinegar or apple cider vinegar

This recipe will need to be started the day before serving.

Add the walnuts to a medium bowl and cover well with filtered or purified water – although this is discarded, the nuts will swell with water and once dehydrated you don't want to leave any chemicals or toxins behind – stir through half the salt and set aside overnight.

Preheat the oven to 80°C conventional.

Drain the walnuts, rinse and pat dry with a clean tea towel. Spread out in a single layer on a baking tray, sprinkle over the remaining salt and place in the oven for about 8 hours, sprinkling over the vinegar for the last hour of drying.

Store the walnuts in an airtight container somewhere cool or refrigerate.

MAKES 500 G

ACTIVATING NUTS AND SEEDS

Most plants have toxic defence mechanisms, survival methods honed over time to protect them from predators. These might be as simple as the leaves of a plant being bitter, discouraging animals from eating any further, to ones with slightly more catastrophic results. Common defences make a plant less digestible to larger predators, and help to bind to nutrients, ultimately making them less valued food sources. Aside from the outright poisonous, most of these defences are tolerated reasonably well by humans, but they do still affect us, and can cause anything from stomach upset to extreme food intolerance.

Additionally, seeds and nuts are armed with enzyme inhibitors that stop them germinating in inhospitable places, as well as energy stores that are pretty indigestible to most creatures – a way of surviving an animal's digestive tract to power growth once they see the light of day. All of these little biological devices can make seeds, nuts and whole grains a little hard to properly digest and a host of their impressive array of nutritional benefits largely unavailable.

One time-honoured way around this problem is to trick the seed or nut into thinking that it's a good time to germinate; when this occurs, it drops its guard and focuses all energy on sprouting. Soaking seeds and nuts in lightly salted water, generally overnight, does the trick. All that's then needed is a long slow dehydration in a low oven or dehydrator until they feel and taste dry – time will vary depending on the nut or seed and the temperature used. Soaking whole grains has a similar effect, simply acidulate the soaking water with a little lemon juice or whey and leave overnight before using.

SPICED SALTS

Flavoured salts are very simple but very effective tools. Use them to build layers of flavour while you're cooking, or to lift a dish just before serving. These salts are very versatile and are used throughout the book, but try different combinations of spices, peel, herbs and any other dehydrated flavourings that take your fancy.

*This seasoning is particularly versatile when working with Chinese themed dishes. Sprinkle it over dumplings, roast duck, pork or fish. I also use this with **Fried Soft-boiled Eggs** (page 75), **Cured Ocean Trout with Wonton Crackers** (page 116), **Prawn & Mushroom Spring Rolls** (page 132), **Stir-fried Pork & Prawn Wontons** (page 162), **Congee** (page 172) and **Fisherman's Basket** (page 228). For more information on Sichuan peppercorns, see page 117.*

SICHUAN & MANDARIN SALT

peel from 3 mandarins
3 tablespoons Sichuan
  peppercorns
1 tablespoon fennel seeds
2½ tablespoons salt flakes
½ teaspoon Chinese
  five-spice

To make the mandarin powder, dehydrate the peel on a baking tray in a 100°C conventional oven for 2–3 hours until brittle.

Blitz the dried peel in a spice grinder, or pound using a mortar and pestle until a powder. Tip into a small bowl.

Toast the Sichuan peppercorns in a dry frying pan over medium heat until fragrant and slightly coloured, about 2 minutes.

Blitz or pound the fennel seeds and peppercorns to a powder and add to a bowl with the salt, five-spice and 1 tablespoon of the mandarin powder. Combine, breaking down the salt flakes a little in the process. Store in a small jar or airtight container.

MAKES ABOUT 70 G

Dukkah

*Sichuan &
Mandarin Salt*

*Coriander & Black
Pepper Salt*

*Celery & Black
Pepper Salt*

*Use this celery salt on sashimi-style tuna or kingfish, **Sweet Potato Chips** (page 126), **Pan con Tomate with Soft-boiled Eggs** (page 71) or in a virgin or bloody mary.*

CELERY & BLACK PEPPER SALT

⅓ cup salt flakes
1 tablespoon celery seeds
2 teaspoons freshly ground black pepper

Blitz all the ingredients in a spice grinder, or pound using a mortar and pestle until a coarse powder. Store in a small jar or airtight container.

MAKES ABOUT 60 G

*This salt is perfect for seasoning stir-fried beef, roasted root vegetables, pork or fish. Try it with my **Roasted Whole Snapper** on pages 222–3.*

CORIANDER & BLACK PEPPER SALT

⅓ cup salt flakes
⅓ cup coriander seeds
1 tablespoon freshly ground black pepper

Blitz all the ingredients in a spice grinder, or pound using a mortar and pestle until a coarse powder. Store in a small jar or airtight container.

MAKES ABOUT 65 G

SPICES

Having a range of spices on hand is an essential part of any good pantry, but it's best not to stock up too much. All spices and dried herbs will become less intense over time, and degrade even more rapidly unless stored in airtight containers in a cool and dark place. I always buy spices in quantities that I will use in a reasonably short period of time. If there's no aroma left in the spices, they're not going to add anything to the dish, and if you're working from a recipe, the specified quantities will be meaningless. Storing them well yourself is important, but it's just as important to buy good spices in the first place. Skip the supermarket and go to Asian, Indian and Middle Eastern grocers for these, their turnover will be better as their customers appreciate and demand freshness.

Many recipes call for toasting spices, which liberates the essential oils and rounds out the flavour, but be careful as you can easily take them too far. While the aroma lifting out of the pan might be great, you don't want all that flavour expended before you actually use them. Over-toasted spices will yield a flat result or, at their worst, impart a burnt character with no spice notes at all.

Try incorporating spices into your everyday cooking: rub a chicken with cumin and garlic before roasting to transform the weekly roast, try some caraway seeds with roasted carrots, some smashed fennel seeds with steamed mussels and tomato, or make up some spiced salts (page 24 and above) to add an instant flavour boost to all kinds of dishes.

*Dukkah is a spice and nut mix of Egyptian origin, and is typically eaten by dipping soft bread first in oil and then into the mix. This version calls for both ground and whole spices, building texture and a more complete flavour expression. Serve it with some good oil, pide or **Simit** (page 88), hard salty cheese and olives and you've got a great snack or appetiser. It's also brilliant scattered over eggs, tossed with roasted brussels sprouts and a little honey, with roasted carrots and parsnips, or with my **Egg, Eggplant & Olive Salad** on page 108. A nicely wrapped jar of homemade dukkah also makes a great gift.*

DUKKAH

150 g pistachio kernels, roughly chopped

150 g toasted blanched almonds, crushed

2 tablespoons sesame seeds

2 tablespoons coriander seeds, lightly crushed

2 tablespoons ground coriander

1 tablespoon ground cumin

2 teaspoons nigella seeds

1 teaspoon caraway seeds

1 teaspoon cumin seeds

1 teaspoon ground turmeric

½ teaspoon chilli powder

½ teaspoon freshly ground black pepper

2 pinches of ground cardamom

Combine all the ingredients well in a bowl. Store in an airtight container in a cool dark place.

MAKES ABOUT 500 G

Ricotta is one of my favourite ingredients. I always seek out the freshest from a trusted deli, and stay well clear of the tubs at the supermarket. Making your own cuts out any doubts about the quality and freshness. It's really a very simple process and, like all things that you probably thought you couldn't make at home, it's incredibly satisfying. Simply spreading it on toasted sourdough with chopped soft herbs and good peppery oil is pretty hard to beat, but to really showcase your efforts, try my Ricotta Ravioli (page 174) or Kale & Spinach Gnudi (page 178). And don't throw out the leftover whey, it can be used for lacto-fermenting vegetables, in bread making, or for adding to soaking legumes and grains to make them more readily digestible and nutritious (see page 23).

FRESH RICOTTA

2 litres full-cream milk
500 ml buttermilk
1½ teaspoons salt flakes

Add all the ingredients to a medium saucepan and heat until just under the boil. Turn the heat to low and simmer very gently for about 5 minutes until there is a clear separation of the curds from the whey. Turn off the heat and stand for a couple of minutes.

Line a large strainer with a few layers of muslin and stand over a large bowl. Spoon the curds into the strainer and set aside for 20 minutes to drain off the excess whey. The ricotta is now ready to use, or refrigerate for later use. For a firmer curd, but lower yield, leave the ricotta in the muslin and squeeze out the moisture regularly over a few hours.

MAKES 500–550 G

There really is no need to buy mayonnaise; it's so easy to whip up a quick one with one egg yolk, a little mustard, salt and pepper and enough oil whisked in to thicken. But if you make a big batch like this, you can have it on hand to use in sandwiches and salads, or to turn into any number of flavoured sauces, from a classic tartare to **Paprika Aioli** *(page 126),* **Sesame Mayonnaise** *(page 137) or* **Nori Tartare** *(page 228), or simply stir through some chilli sauce or* **Gochujang Chilli Sauce** *(page 40) for a quick spicy dipping sauce. This recipe makes quite a thick mayonnaise, ready to be thinned down with other flavour additions or a spoonful of sour cream or yoghurt to lighten and add a little sharpness.*

MASTER MAYONNAISE

4 extra-large egg yolks
1½ tablespoons Dijon mustard
1½ tablespoons white wine vinegar
salt flakes and freshly ground black pepper
350 ml extra-virgin olive oil
300 ml grapeseed oil (or other neutral oil)
juice of 1 large lemon (2½–3 tablespoons)

Add the egg yolks, mustard, vinegar and 1 teaspoon of salt to a food processor and process until combined. Gradually pour in the oils while processing – it should take about 5 minutes to add and emulsify all the oil.

Mix in the lemon juice, season with pepper and a little more salt if necessary and transfer to an airtight container. Press a layer of plastic wrap directly on top of the mayonnaise to stop a skin forming and seal with the lid. The mayonnaise will keep for up to 10 days as long as it is well sealed and refrigerated.

MAKES ABOUT 800 G

*I much prefer to use red onions rather than brown for this jam. They add such a beautifully vibrant purple tone to the finished preserve, and their natural sweetness is a perfect match to the subtle tang of the fino sherry and sherry vinegar. This is great with pâtés, terrines, a jaffle with cheddar, a rare roast beef sandwich, or even as a filling component for a tart or quiche. Try it with my **Chicken Liver Parfait** (page 202), or with some sharp cheddar and **Oatcakes** (page 80).*

RED ONION & SHERRY JAM

1 tablespoon grapeseed oil (or other neutral oil)

8 red onions, halved and sliced lengthways

2 garlic cloves, smashed

1 tablespoon salt flakes

1 handful of golden raisins

½ teaspoon black peppercorns, cracked

1 teaspoon allspice berries

1 teaspoon coriander seeds, lightly ground

1 fresh bay leaf

2 bird's eye chillies, split lengthways

120 g caster sugar

100 g brown sugar

150 ml white wine vinegar

100 ml sherry vinegar

2½ tablespoons fino sherry

You will need enough sterilised jars and lids (see page 17) for 3½ cups of onion jam.

Heat the oil in a wide, heavy-based saucepan over medium heat. Add the onion, garlic and salt and cook, stirring frequently, for 5 minutes. Add the raisins, pepper, spices, bay leaf and chillies, cover, turn the heat to low and cook for 15 minutes, stirring occasionally.

Add the sugars and vinegars to the pan and bring to the boil. Simmer, stirring frequently, for about 20 minutes until all the liquid has evaporated and the onion is stewed and sticky but still moist – it should still be vibrantly coloured. Stir through the sherry and remove from the heat.

Spoon the jam into jars while hot, seal and turn upside down to cool. You can use the jam immediately, but it's better after a week and will store for up to 3 months in the pantry. Refrigerate after opening and keep for up to 2 weeks.

MAKES 3½ CUPS

*This sweet and spicy plum sauce is perfect with fried wontons, pork spare ribs, roast duck, **Prawn & Mushroom Spring Rolls** (page 132), **Spiced Pork Belly Bao** (page 137) or **Bánh Mì** (pages 146–7). Make this when plums are abundant, and while you can use any type of plum, blood plums are ideal, and they add such great colour, too.*

SPICED BLOOD PLUM SAUCE

2.5 kg blood plums, stoned and roughly chopped

400 g red onion, finely diced

6 large garlic cloves, finely grated

120 g ginger, finely grated

3 long red chillies, sliced

1 litre malt vinegar

700 g brown sugar

500 g caster sugar

2 fresh bay leaves

6 star anise

1 tablespoon ground ginger

2 tablespoons brown mustard seeds

1 tablespoon chilli flakes

⅓ cup salt flakes

2 tablespoons shrimp paste

300 g tamarind puree

You will need enough sterilised jars and lids (see page 17) for 2 litres of plum sauce. You will need to start this recipe the day before serving.

Add all the ingredients except the shrimp paste and tamarind puree to a large, wide-based saucepan. Bring to a simmer and cook for 1½ hours.

Wrap the shrimp paste in foil and toast in a frying pan over low heat or in a moderate (180°C conventional) oven for a few minutes.

After 1½ hours, add the shrimp paste and tamarind puree to the pan, stir through and cook for about 25 minutes until the sauce is thick and syrupy.

Spoon the hot sauce into the hot jars and seal immediately. Flip the jars onto their lids and set aside to cool. Use the plum sauce after 24 hours and store unopened for around 2 months. Refrigerate after opening and keep for up to 2 weeks.

MAKES 2 LITRES

Pickled watermelon rind is a real specialty of the American South, and a pretty ingenious – and delicious – way of using something that would otherwise go to waste. Slice the pickled rind finely and serve with charcuterie, on a ploughman's platter, with a Christmas ham, in salads or even with a curry. And don't forget to eat the flesh!

WATERMELON RIND PICKLE

1 × 4 kg watermelon (2.5 kg watermelon rind)

½ cup rock salt

PICKLING LIQUID

1 kg caster sugar

1.2 litres white wine vinegar

800 ml water

1 lemon, finely sliced

3 star anise

6 green cardamom pods, smashed

12 allspice berries

1 tablespoon Sichuan peppercorns

2 teaspoons black peppercorns

1 cinnamon stick

You will need two sterilised 1.5-litre jars with lids (see page 17) for this recipe.

Cut the watermelon into quarters. Cut the flesh away from the rind, leaving about 5 mm of pink flesh attached. Cut the rind into large even chunks.

Add the salt and 5 litres of water to a large saucepan and bring to the boil. Add the rind, cover with a plate to keep it submerged, and simmer for 10 minutes. Strain off the liquid and plunge the rind into iced water to stop the cooking process.

Boil the pickling liquid ingredients in a large saucepan for 5 minutes, stirring until the sugar dissolves.

Drain the rind and add it to the boiling pickling liquid. Bring back to the boil and cook for 10 minutes.

Divide the rind and liquid between the hot jars, seal tightly, turn upside down and set aside to cool. Refrigerate to store. Use after 1 day and keep for up to 3 months.

MAKES 2 × 1.5-LITRE JARS

This is a versatile chilli sauce using the Korean fermented chilli condiment gochujang. It's best eaten within a week to keep the vibrant flavour of the garlic and ginger, but it will certainly keep for longer – not that it lasts that long in my house. Stir it through a lemon juice and extra-virgin olive oil vinaigrette and drizzle over fish; add it to **Fried Soft-boiled Eggs** *(page 75); use it with* **Spiced Pork Belly Bao** *(page 137),* **Bibimbap** *(page 171),* **Congee** *(page 172) or* **Bo Ssam** *(pages 232–3); stir it through a bowl of noodles or broth; or simply serve it as a hotly sweet and earthy universal condiment.*

GOCHUJANG CHILLI SAUCE

2 garlic cloves, finely grated

8-cm piece of ginger, finely grated

½ cup gochujang (see below)

3 tablespoons white miso paste

2 tablespoons pure maple syrup

1½ tablespoons rice vinegar

1 tablespoon grapeseed oil (or other neutral oil)

1 tablespoon sesame oil

1½ tablespoons sesame seeds

Add all the ingredients to a medium bowl and combine, adding a little water if the mix is too stiff. Use immediately or refrigerate for up to 1 week.

MAKES ABOUT 1 CUP

GOCHUJANG

Gochujang is a fermented paste made from red chillies, rice and soybeans and, like gochugaru (see page 47), is an essential ingredient in Korean cuisine. Both gochujang and gochugaru were traditionally made in the home, and it's really not that long since commercial production has taken over the task. Gochujang is hot with earthy, umami notes and subtle fermented funk.

*This sweet and smoky chilli relish is great in braises (see pages 236–7 for my **Pulled Pork Belly with Tortillas**), stirred through **Mayonnaise** (page 31) or dressings, as a condiment for tacos, barbecued meat or chicken, with fried eggs or in a **Jaffle** (see page 64 for other jaffle ideas) – the possibilities really are endless. This will keep well if bottled carefully, and will last for a couple of months refrigerated once opened.*

SMOKY CHIPOTLE ADOBO

20 chipotle chillies (dried, smoked jalepeños)

20 ancho chillies (dried poblanos)

2 onions, roughly diced

12 garlic cloves

2 tablespoons dried Mexican or Greek oregano

6 thyme sprigs, leaves stripped and chopped

2 fresh bay leaves

3 teaspoons cumin seeds

3 teaspoons coriander seeds

80 ml extra-virgin olive oil

350 ml white wine vinegar

100 ml balsamic vinegar

150 g brown sugar

800 g passata

2½ tablespoons salt flakes

You will need enough sterilised jars and lids (see page 17) for 2 litres of chipotle sauce. This recipe can easily be halved, but it keeps well, is great to have on hand, and little jars also make nice gifts.

Wash the chillies in cold water and trim off the stems. Place in a large saucepan, cover with boiling water and simmer for about 15 minutes until the chillies are soft. Drain and rinse away most of the seeds.

Add the onion, garlic, herbs, spices and 200 ml of water to a blender and blitz to a smooth puree. Add the reconstituted chillies and roughly blitz to a chunky sauce.

Place a large, heavy-based saucepan over high heat. Add the oil and chilli puree and cook, stirring constantly, for 3–4 minutes. Add the white wine vinegar, balsamic, sugar, passata and salt and simmer gently for 30 minutes.

Adjust the seasoning if necessary and spoon the hot sauce into the hot jars. Seal the jars immediately, flip on their lids and set aside to cool. Once bottled, the sauce will keep for up to 6 months, but needs to be refrigerated after opening.

MAKES 2 LITRES

Smokey chipotle adobo,

20 chipotle chillies
20 ancho chillies
2 brown onions
12 garlic cloves
2 tablespoon
6 thyme
2 Bay leaves
3⊕ cumin
3⊕ coriander
80 ml extra virgin
350 ml w/wine vin
150 g Brown sugar
800 ml passata.

NOT SO HOT

Chilli-derived heat is a pretty important part of Mexican cuisine, but the distinctive flavour of each of the dazzling array of local peppers is just as critical, especially when you add in the richly smoky tones of the dried versions. Dried ancho, pasilla and guajillo chillies are not especially hot but they are rich with character, containing berry, raisin, brown sugar, cocoa, green tea, prune and even tobacco flavours. These chillies, amongst others, are used to build the many flavour layers of the country's famous chocolate-laced *moles*. A good range of dried chillies can be increasingly found in specialist grocers and online.

Spiced Chinese Pickles

The first time I went to Kylie Kwong's restaurant, Billy Kwong, many years ago back in its old Crown Street site, the first thing I ate was a plate of wontons with pickles, and I was instantly hooked. It's taken me a surprisingly long time to make them myself, but I love them just as much as I did back then. These are great with a cold beer, or can be chopped and used in salads. I also use them to provide a sweetly sour balance to all manner of dishes: **Fried Soft-boiled Eggs** *(page 75),* **Prawn & Mushroom Spring Rolls** *(page 132),* **Bánh Mì** *(pages 146–7),* **Lamb Ribs** *(page 150),* **Congee** *(page 172),* **Fisherman's Basket** *(page 228) and* **Bo Ssam** *(pages 232–3).*

SPICED CHINESE PICKLES

4 Lebanese cucumbers, split lengthways and cut into 1-cm slices

1 celery heart and surrounding inner stalks, yellow leaves attached, cut into 1.5-cm slices on an angle

1 daikon, peeled and cut into 5-mm thick discs

½ wombok, shredded 2-cm wide on an angle

1 fennel bulb, finely shaved lengthways

1 bunch of red radishes, trimmed and quartered

½ cup salt flakes

2.5 litres white vinegar

800 g caster sugar

6 garlic cloves, smashed

12 × 4-mm slices of ginger

6 small dried chillies

3 teaspoons Sichuan peppercorns

4 star anise

This recipe will need to be started 3 days before serving. You will need six clean jars with lids for the pickles – the jars can be bigger than needed for each pickle, as they don't need to be completely filled.

Add the cucumber, celery, daikon, wombok, fennel and radish to separate bowls or containers and sprinkle a tablespoon of salt over each. Toss the vegetables through the salt, cover and refrigerate overnight.

Add the vinegar and sugar to a medium saucepan and bring to the boil. Stir to dissolve the sugar, turn down the heat and simmer for 30 minutes. Refrigerate until chilled.

The following day, drain the vegetables and squeeze out any excess liquid gently in your hands. Place the vegetables in individual jars and pour over the pickling liquid to cover. Divide the garlic, ginger, chillies and peppercorns between all the jars. Add two star anise to the fennel and two to the cucumber. Refrigerate for 2 days before eating, and keep for 3–4 weeks.

MAKES 6 SMALL JARS

*Kimchi is probably Korea's most famous food product, and its popularity in the west has soared with an increased interest in both Korean cuisine and fermented products. Not that all kimchi has to be buried in the backyard for a couple of months to mature, fresher versions are just as delicious, trading in the funk for a little more brightness and crunch. I like both types, from the pungent and bitey to this one, which fits into a fresher mould. It's up to you, though, if you want a little more funk, leave the jar on the bench to ferment for a day or so, or longer – just make sure the kimchi is submerged in liquid and carefully release the gasses from the jar every now and then. Chilling the kimchi will retard the fermentation, so refrigerate once you're happy with the flavour. It's great in **Bricohe Rolls with Crayfish** (page 140) and **Bo Ssam** (pages 232–3).*

QUICK KIMCHI

1 wombok (about 1.5 kg)

70 g sea salt

3 tablespoons gochugaru (see below)

130 g ginger, finely grated

5 garlic cloves, finely grated

5 long red chillies, deseeded and finely chopped

4 spring onions, white part only, finely sliced

½ bunch of chives, cut into batons

2 tablespoons raw sugar

2 tablespoons light soy sauce

2 tablespoons fish sauce

2 tablespoons dried shrimp, pounded or finely chopped

You will need enough sterilised jars and lids (see page 17) for 4 cups of kimchi.

Quarter the wombok lengthways and slice away the thickest part of the core. Cut the wedges crossways at 4-cm intervals. Rinse well, drain and place in a large bowl.

Dissolve the salt in 200 ml of warm water and pour over the cabbage. Toss thoroughly and set aside for 2 hours.

Drain the wombok, rinse in cold water, drain again and squeeze out a little of the excess liquid.

Add the gochugaru and 2½ tablespoons of warm water to a large bowl and mix into a paste. Add the wombok and toss through until well coated. Add the remaining ingredients and combine thoroughly with your hands for a couple of minutes – use some disposable gloves for this, as the chillies will burn.

Pack the kimchi firmly into the jars, leaving a 3-cm headspace at the top, and cover with the liquid in the bowl. Cap and refrigerate. The kimchi is ready now, but it will intensify in flavour over time, and will keep for about 1 month.

MAKES ABOUT 4 CUPS

GOCHUGARU

Gochugaru is Korean chilli powder, and an essential ingredient in Korean cuisine that can't be substituted with other versions. The best gochugaru is made from sun-dried, deseeded chillies and is vibrantly red, which adds distinctive colour and a sweetness that underpins the heat. The intensity of the heat can vary, and English labelling is not always terribly reliable, so it's often best to stick to a brand that you like to keep the spiciness in check.

Quick Kimchi

*I've been curing sides of ocean trout and salmon for as long as I can remember. They've featured on my menus, and I can't remember a Christmas when I haven't presented a whole side with a spread of accompaniments. It's really a very simple process and is so much better, and cheaper, than commercial versions – especially the generic smoked stuff. I usually serve the sliced fish with things like diced shallots, crème fraîche, pickled beetroot, dill and horseradish, but by tweaking the cure and sprinkling over some Sichuan pepper and dried mandarin powder the rich oiliness of the trout is just as delicious paired with Asian flavours. Try it with wonton crackers and sesame mayonnaise (page 116) or poached eggs and **Gochujang Chilli Sauce** (page 40), in a sandwich with cucumber and hard-boiled egg, or even with some rye or pumpernickel and crème fraîche.*

CITRUS-CURED OCEAN TROUT WITH SICHUAN PEPPER, MANDARIN & SESAME

1 × 1.2–1.5 kg side of ocean trout (or salmon), skin on, trimmed and pin-boned

1 tablespoon extra-virgin olive oil

½ teaspoon sesame oil

CURE

finely grated zest and juice of 2 lemons and 2 limes (about 200 ml juice)

200 g rock salt

100 g caster sugar

10 g (2 tablespoons) coriander seeds, lightly ground

10 g (2 tablespoons) Sichuan peppercorns, lightly ground

5 g (1 heaped teaspoon) white peppercorns, lightly ground

SICHUAN & MANDARIN POWDER

peel from 3 mandarins

1½ tablespoons Sichuan peppercorns, toasted

2 teaspoons white peppercorns

Line a large ceramic dish or deep tray with plastic wrap, leaving enough overhanging to wrap the trout. Press any joins together to ensure that it doesn't leak.

For the cure, add all the ingredients to a medium bowl and mix until well combined. Tip half the cure into the dish or tray and place the trout on top, skin-side down, ensuring that the slurry is evenly distributed under the fish. Tip the remaining cure over the top of the fish and distribute reasonably evenly. Bring the edges of the wrap together and seal. Place in the refrigerator for 24 hours, opening the parcel at the halfway mark to flip the trout.

Meanwhile, to make the mandarin powder, dehydrate the mandarin peel on a baking tray in a 100°C conventional oven for 2–3 hours until brittle. Blitz the peel in a spice grinder, or pound using a mortar and pestle until a powder. Blitz the Sichuan and white peppercorns and 1 tablespoon of the mandarin powder until fine. Store in a small dry jar or container until needed.

After 24 hours, remove the trout from the cure and wipe down with paper towel.

Combine the olive and sesame oils in a small bowl and brush over the flesh of the trout. Coat with most of the Sichuan mandarin powder, wrap tightly in plastic wrap and refrigerate for 1 hour before using. The trout will keep for 10 days wrapped and refrigerated.

SERVES 10–12

There are few things more nourishing than a good chicken broth, but you're only getting part of the health benefits if you cook your stock for a few hours. Cooking the stock overnight extracts so much more from the bones and joints, pulling out collagen, calcium and other minerals in easily absorbed forms. It also makes a densely flavoured stock that gels incredibly well. Use this whenever you would normally use chicken stock, or have a hot cup as a snack. I happily drink it just with a little seasoning, and the girls love it with some miso and dried wakame stirred through – for breakfast, would you believe!

As the point is to extract everything from the bones, I really recommend sourcing the best chicken bones and bits that you can: definitely genuine free range, and preferably organic and pasture raised. Freeze the leftover bones from the weekly roast and toss them in the pot too, or cover the bones from a roast chicken with water, throw in a few aromatic vegetables and let it tick over slowly overnight for an easy version. The ingredients listed below are ideal, but if you omit the necks, feet and giblets and make up the difference with more bones, the broth will still turn out well.

CHICKEN BONE BROTH

5 chicken frames
3 onions, skin on, cut in half
2 garlic bulbs, cut in half
  horizontally
1 kg chicken feet
1 kg chicken necks
500 g chicken giblets (optional)
4 large carrots, cut in half
2 leeks, trimmed and split in half
½ head of celery, roughly
  chopped
4 fresh bay leaves
1 tablespoon black peppercorns
125 ml apple cider vinegar
1 handful of thyme sprigs
1 bunch of parsley stalks

Preheat the oven to 220°C fan-forced (240°C conventional).

Add the chicken frames, onion and garlic to a roasting tray and roast for 30 minutes.

Tip the contents of the roasting tray, including any juices, into a large stockpot – about 20-litre capacity. (If you don't have a stockpot this large, either halve the recipe or use multiple pots.) Add the feet, necks and giblets (if using), cover with about 12 litres of water (filtered or purified if possible) and bring up to a simmer. Regularly skim off any impurities as they rise to the surface over about 15 minutes or so. Add the carrot, leek, celery, bay leaves, peppercorns and vinegar and bring back up to a simmer. Reduce the heat so that the water is barely ticking over and skim again regularly until clear of foam or impurities – do this frequently to start with and revisit every now and then. Cook for about 24 hours, topping up with a little water if necessary. Add the thyme for the last 3 hours of cooking, and the parsley stalks for the last 30 minutes.

Turn the heat off and stand for 30 minutes before straining through a fine sieve. Portion the broth into handy quantities and cool a little before freezing or refrigerating.

MAKES ABOUT 10 LITRES

PUT A FOOT IN IT

When the trolley laden with chicken feet rolls around at yum cha it usually gets pretty definitive reactions – there are very few people who are lukewarm on the subject of sucking on the feet of fowl. But if you're one of the people who waves the trolley on, please don't be too queasy about using them for broth. The feet are full of collagen, trace minerals and other compounds that can be beneficial for our own wellbeing and joint health. The huge mass of collagen that they contain also helps a stock to gel incredibly well. Animal collagen is basically where we get gelatine from, and provides binding qualities to all kinds of things, from Aeroplane Jelly to glue. Besides being an aid to good joint health, it also has a pretty important culinary advantage: stocks that gel well are brilliant to use in sauces, giving them viscosity and a luscious intensity that is hard to mimic.

BREAKFAST IS KING

JUMP THE WEEKEND CAFE QUEUES

**BANANA HOTCAKES WITH BACON
& MISO–MAPLE BUTTER**

SISTERLY BANANA BREAD

**ROSEWATER HOTCAKES WITH ROASTED
RHUBARB & STRAWBERRY**

JAFFLES WITH JARLSBERG SAUCE & CORN

**GOLDEN POTATO WAFFLES WITH SMOKED
TROUT, SOUR SHERRY ONIONS & HORSERADISH**

**RYE TOAST WITH AVOCADO, POACHED EGG,
CHILLI & LAVA SALT**

**PAN CON TOMATE WITH SOFT-BOILED
EGGS & CELERY SALT**

HUEVOS A LA FLAMENCA

**FRIED SOFT-BOILED EGGS WITH OYSTER SAUCE,
THAI BASIL, CHILLI & PICKLES**

The savoury, umami-rich note of miso really sings with the bacon, banana and maple syrup, and the moist hotcakes just soak up all the delicious flavours. Please use good free-range bacon for this, and if you can source quality dry-cured rashers, all the better. This recipe can be halved.

BANANA HOTCAKES WITH BACON & MISO–MAPLE BUTTER

450 ml milk
60 g unsalted butter, melted
2 eggs, separated
1 teaspoon vanilla extract
300 g plain flour
80 g caster sugar
3 teaspoons baking powder
2 pinches of salt
2 large ripe bananas, sliced
8 rashers of premium bacon
pure maple syrup, to serve

MISO–MAPLE BUTTER
140 g butter, at room
  temperature
2 tablespoons pure maple syrup
2 heaped tablespoons white
  miso paste

Preheat the oven to 180°C fan-forced (200°C conventional). Line a baking tray with baking paper.

For the miso–maple butter, add all the ingredients to a medium bowl and whisk vigorously until combined. Use as is, or chill for later use.

For the hotcakes, add the milk, melted butter, egg yolks and vanilla to a jug and stir until combined.

Add the eggwhites to a medium bowl and whisk until fluffy.

Dry whisk the flour, sugar, baking powder and salt in a large bowl to break up any clumps. Make a well in the centre and add the milk mix while whisking constantly to form a smooth batter. Using a spatula, carefully fold in the whipped eggwhite until combined.

Preheat two small, ovenproof frying pans in the oven for 2 minutes. Grease with a little butter or spray with oil and add a quarter of the batter to each pan. Divide a quarter of the banana between the two pans and bake for about 10 minutes until lightly golden.

Meanwhile, place four bacon rashers on the prepared tray and bake until cooked to your liking.

Once the hotcakes are cooked, loosen the edges and slip onto warm plates. Finish with another quarter of the banana, top with bacon, dress with some miso butter and serve with maple syrup.

Repeat for the remaining hotcakes.

SERVES 4

Sisterly Banana Bread

*My pastry chef sister, Odette, was kind enough to give me this recipe – potentially after a little sisterly pressure. This is really somewhere between banana bread and cake, with a super moist and finely textured crumb. Eat this just as is on the day of baking, or try a slice with a drizzle of **Miso–Maple Butter** (page 57).*

SISTERLY BANANA BREAD

100 ml extra-virgin olive oil

1 × 70 g egg

50 g natural yoghurt

2 g (¼ teaspoon) salt

170 g plain flour

4 g (1 teaspoon) baking powder

4 g (1 teaspoon) bicarbonate of soda

200 g pureed banana, plus 1 sliced banana

110 g caster sugar

Preheat the oven to 170°C fan-forced (190°C conventional). Grease a 25-cm loaf tin and line with baking paper.

Combine the oil, egg, yoghurt and salt in a small bowl.

Add the flour, baking powder and bicarbonate of soda to a medium bowl and dry whisk to remove any clumps.

Add the pureed banana and sugar to the bowl of a stand mixer and beat on medium with the paddle attachment until incorporated. Turn the mixer to low and gradually add the oil mix until incorporated. Add the flour mix and beat for 3 minutes until incorporated.

Tip the mix into the prepared tin, top with the sliced banana and bake for 25–30 minutes until cooked – the cooked cake will be springy to the touch, and a skewer will come out clean. Set aside to cool in the tin before unmoulding.

SERVES 6–8

This is a pretty tricked up breakfast – perfect for those who think dessert usually comes too late in the day. You could make these hotcakes even more indulgent with a scoop of ice cream, or skip the fancy toppings and just dress them with a little brown sugar, a generous squeeze of lemon and some yoghurt. You can also cook the mix in a bigger pan and make two large hotcakes to share, or halve the recipe if your needs aren't as great.

ROSEWATER HOTCAKES WITH ROASTED RHUBARB & STRAWBERRY

450 ml milk

60 g unsalted butter, melted

2 eggs, separated

1 teaspoon vanilla extract

300 g plain flour

80 g caster sugar

3 teaspoons baking powder

2 pinches of salt flakes

thick natural yoghurt, to serve

2 handfuls of bright green pistachio kernels, smashed using a mortar and pestle

pashmak (Persian fairy floss), to serve (optional)

ROASTED RHUBARB & STRAWBERRY

1 bunch of young rhubarb, trimmed and cut into 3-cm lengths

250 g strawberries, whole and unhulled

130 g caster sugar

2 teaspoons rosewater

Preheat the oven to 180°C fan-forced (200°C conventional).

For the roasted rhubarb, add the rhubarb, strawberries and sugar to a large ceramic or enamel baking dish, toss briefly and spread out evenly. Set aside for 10 minutes before roasting in the oven for 20 minutes.

Tip the strawberries, rhubarb and any syrup into a large bowl, pour over the rosewater and set aside.

For the hotcakes, add the milk, melted butter, egg yolks and vanilla to a jug and stir until combined.

Add the eggwhites to a medium bowl and whisk until fluffy.

Dry whisk the flour, sugar, baking powder and salt in a large bowl to break up any clumps. Make a well in the centre and add the milk mix while whisking constantly to form a smooth batter. Using a spatula, carefully fold in the whipped eggwhite until combined.

Preheat two small, ovenproof frying pans in the oven for 2 minutes. Grease with a little butter or spray with oil and add a quarter of the batter to each pan. Bake for 10 minutes until lightly golden. Once cooked, loosen the edges and slip the hotcakes onto warm plates. Repeat for the remaining batter.

Dress the hotcakes with the roasted strawberries and rhubarb, drizzle over some syrup and dollop on some yoghurt. Finish with the pistachios and pashmak (if using).

SERVES 4

Rosewater Hotcakes with Roasted Rhubarb & Strawberry

*I ate many a jaffle growing up, but the old Martini repertoire didn't really stretch past baked beans with egg or cheese. Well, dad used to make them with cold bolognaise and egg, but we used to turn our noses up at that – sorry, Dad, you were right about that one. Whether using up some leftover **Bolognaise-style Mushroom Ragu** (page 180) or **Sausage Ragu** (page 213) with some torn buffalo mozzarella, making this creamy corn version from scratch, or exploring other combinations, the possibilities are almost endless. You could use this cheesy sauce with some tuna for a pretty spectacular tuna melt, or even try a sweet jaffle with mashed banana and chocolate, if that's more your thing.*

JAFFLES WITH JARLSBERG SAUCE & CORN

1 tablespoon extra-virgin olive oil
1 garlic clove, sliced
3 corn cobs, kernels sliced off
1 long green chilli, finely chopped
salt flakes and freshly ground black pepper
2 pinches of caster sugar
½ teaspoon smoked paprika
1 handful of coriander leaves
butter
16 slices of white bread

JARLSBERG SAUCE
400 ml milk
25 g butter
1½ tablespoons plain flour
1 pinch of salt flakes
160 g Jarlsberg cheese, diced

You will need a jaffle maker for this recipe.

Heat the oil in a large frying pan over medium heat. Add the garlic and fry for about 2 minutes until fragrant. Add the corn and chilli, season and cook for 10 minutes over low heat, stirring occasionally. Stir in the sugar and paprika and cook for a minute or so. Stir through the coriander and take off the heat.

For the Jarlsberg sauce, add the milk to a small saucepan, bring to a simmer and turn off the heat.

Melt the butter in a medium saucepan over medium heat. Add the flour and stir continuously for 2 minutes. Whisk in the warm milk to form a smooth sauce. Add the salt and cook for 4 minutes until thickened and silky. Add the cheese and stir over low heat until melted. Take off the heat and cool.

Butter one side of each slice of bread. Place a slice of bread, buttered side down, in each jaffle bay and spoon on some sauce. Follow with some corn and top with another slice of bread, buttered side up. Cook until golden and repeat.

MAKES 8

A waffle maker is a foolproof way to make a perfectly golden and crunchy roesti. Although this combination of smoked trout, horseradish, sweetly sour onions and crunchy raw beetroot is pretty hard to beat, you can swap in anything you like: smoked salmon, crème fraîche, dill and some finely diced shallots; smoked eel, pickled beetroot and horseradish cream; or even go super decadent and serve with caviar and traditional accompaniments. You can also cut the waffle into four and serve this as a canapé.

GOLDEN POTATO WAFFLES WITH SMOKED TROUT, SOUR SHERRY ONIONS & HORSERADISH

1 kg Kennebec potatoes (or any good chipper), peeled

2 tablespoons grated fresh horseradish (or unsweetened prepared horseradish)

3 tablespoons thick sour cream

50 g plain flour

80 ml extra-virgin olive oil, plus extra to serve

salt flakes and freshly ground black pepper

2 baby watermelon beetroots

1 side of hot-smoked trout

2 handfuls of chervil

lemon wedges, to serve

SOUR SHERRY ONIONS

2 red onions, finely sliced

2 ½ tablespoons sherry vinegar

2 tablespoons caster sugar

½ teaspoon salt flakes

You will need a waffle maker for this recipe.

Add the potatoes to a saucepan of cold salted water over high heat and bring to the boil. Turn down the heat and simmer for 5 minutes. Drain and set aside until just cool enough to handle.

For the sour onions, add all the ingredients to a medium saucepan over medium heat. Cover and cook for 15 minutes, stirring occasionally, until softened and vibrantly pink. Set aside to cool.

Combine the horseradish and sour cream in a small bowl and refrigerate until needed.

Coarsely grate the potatoes onto a tray and divide into four even portions. Add 1 tablespoon of flour and 1 tablespoon of oil to one of the portions and season with salt and pepper – depending on your waffle maker, make one or more at a time, but only flour each portion just before cooking – and combine gently by mixing with open fingers. Shape into a loosely formed cake, add to the waffle maker and cook until golden. You can keep the cooked waffles warm in a low oven if necessary.

Meanwhile, trim the beetroots leaving a little of the stem on and wash thoroughly to dislodge any dirt. Slice finely lengthways using a mandoline.

Top each waffle with some sour onions, a dollop of horseradish cream, flakes of trout, slices of beetroot and fine sprigs of chervil. Drizzle over a little oil and serve with lemon wedges on the side.

SERVES 4

This is a very regular breakfast for me, and sometimes it's not the prettiest affair when I'm in a rush – but it's always delicious. Avocado on toast is such a cafe favourite, and not just locally. A few years back, I ordered avocado on toast at New York's popular Cafe Gitane, and when it arrived it seemed I wasn't alone, every single table had a plate of toast smeared with vibrant avocado and flecked with chilli flakes. Use a ripe, unblemished avocado, good-quality bread, fresh peppery oil and the best eggs you can find – and don't forget the lemon! Also, if you've got any **Turkish-style Roasted Pumpkin & Walnut Dip** *(page 100) left over, try using it instead of avocado.*

RYE TOAST WITH AVOCADO, POACHED EGG, CHILLI & LAVA SALT

2 tablespoons white vinegar

2 very fresh extra-large eggs, at room temperature

2 thick slices of rye bread

1 large avocado

1 teaspoon chilli flakes

½ lemon

1 teaspoon black lava salt

freshly ground black pepper

extra-virgin olive oil, to serve

Bring a medium saucepan of water to a simmer, add the vinegar and stir to create a whirlpool. Crack an egg into a cup or small bowl and carefully tip into the centre of the vortex. Let the egg spin for 1 minute before stirring again and adding the other egg. Cook each egg for 3½ minutes, or until cooked to your liking. Briefly drain off any water on paper towel.

Meanwhile, toast the bread well and smear half the avocado over each slice. Sprinkle the chilli flakes around the edges and top with the poached eggs. Squeeze over some lemon juice, season with the lava salt and some pepper, drizzle over a little oil and serve.

SERVES 2

LAVA SALT

Despite the dramatic name, lava salt is not actually harvested from volcanoes. Rather it is sea salt that has been combined with purified volcanic charcoal to give it a striking appearance. It is said to have some beneficial digestive and detoxifying properties, but I'm in it for the visual impact.

Soft-boiled eggs and soldiers are a pretty good way to start the day. But when tomatoes are in season and deliciously ripe, switching the soldiers for the Catalan specialty pan con tomate *(tomato bread) and adding a sprinkling of homemade* **Celery & Black Pepper Salt** *(page 26) elevates this old-school breakfast into something truly special.*

PAN CON TOMATE WITH SOFT-BOILED EGGS & CELERY SALT

4 extra-large eggs, at room temperature

4 slices of sourdough bread

1 large garlic clove

4 very ripe tomatoes

freshly ground black pepper

2 tablespoons extra-virgin olive oil

1 handful of pale celery heart leaves

3 teaspoons Celery & Black Pepper Salt (page 26)

Carefully lower the eggs into a saucepan of simmering water and cook for 5½ minutes.

Meanwhile, toast or grill the bread until quite firm and a little scorched. Rub each slice of toast vigorously with the garlic. Make an incision in each tomato and rub one on each slice so that the flesh and juice is mostly taken up by the toast. Grind over some pepper and drizzle with the oil.

Lift the eggs from the water, refresh for 40 seconds in cold water and place in eggcups.

Plate the tomato bread, scatter over the celery leaves and serve with the boiled eggs and celery salt.

SERVES 4

EGGS

I'm very fussy about eggs, and I don't mind paying a bit more for the best. Like chicken (see page 145), we've become accustomed to eggs being cheap, but not only do factory farmed eggs taste ordinary, they're also produced by birds that are living miserable lives on a far from natural diet – it's not good for us, and it's not good for the chickens. There has been a real surge in demand for free-range eggs, and unless you're buying accredited free-range eggs or know the supplier, you might be surprised at how flexibly the term is applied. It's not just the stocking density either. Hens are healthier, happier and lay better eggs when they can forage naturally, unearthing worms and bugs and whatever else takes their fancy. Sometimes, lower densities are enough to provide this diversity, but many producers are now taking this a step further and moving the birds around their properties in mobile henhouses. This ensures fresh pasture and a new smorgasbord of bugs, grubs and seeds for the chooks. This type of rearing is often referred to as pasture-raised or pastured, and it's better for the land, better for the bird, better for us, and so much tastier. Just make sure you get what you pay for. Do a little research and be certain that the supplier is doing the right thing – the idyllic picture on the carton doesn't always tell the real story.

My good friend Emma cooked in Barcelona for many years, and this dish of baked eggs was a bit of a favourite breakfast in her restaurant – especially after a big night on the town. This dish, actually a specialty of the southern region of Andalusia (the home of Flamenco), is one that varies greatly from cook to cook, and from day to day. It's principally a delicious way of using up trimmings of jamon, chorizo and the like, combined with whatever vegetables are to hand. Many cooks always use potatoes, but Emma's version calls for chickpeas, and if you want to make it vegetarian, skip the jamon and chorizo and swap in mushrooms, but add a little extra oil. This can be made in one large terracotta dish, or can be divided into individual ramekins.

HUEVOS A LA FLAMENCA

80 ml extra-virgin olive oil

1 white onion, finely diced

2 garlic cloves, crushed with a pinch of salt

150 g jamon, diced

150 g semi-cured chorizo, sliced

1 tablespoon sweet Spanish paprika

2 tablespoons sherry vinegar

6 ripe tomatoes, coarsely grated

2 tablespoons tomato paste

1 × 400 g can chickpeas, drained and well rinsed

150 g green beans, finely sliced

80 g frozen peas

salt flakes

6 piquillo peppers (see below) (or 2 roasted red capsicums), cut into strips

6 eggs

toasted sourdough bread, to serve

PICADO

1 large bunch of flat-leaf parsley, leaves picked and finely chopped

1 garlic clove, crushed

100 ml extra-virgin olive oil

1 teaspoon salt flakes

Preheat the oven to 160°C fan-forced (180°C conventional).

For the picado, add all the ingredients to a small bowl and stir until well combined.

Heat the oil in a large, deep-sided terracotta dish or frying pan over medium heat. Add the onion and garlic and cook until soft and translucent, about 5 minutes. Add the jamon and chorizo and cook for 5 minutes to render out some of the fat. Add the paprika and stir to combine. Deglaze with the sherry vinegar and stir in the tomato and tomato paste. Cook for 10 minutes, stirring frequently. Add the chickpeas, beans, peas and 400 ml of water, season and bring to a simmer. Scatter the peppers on top and take off the heat.

Make six indentations in the mix with a spoon and gently crack in the eggs. Cover with foil, being careful not to touch the yolks, and bake for 7 minutes. Uncover and bake for a further 2–4 minutes until the eggs are cooked to your liking.

Serve straight from the oven with the picado and some toasted bread on the side.

SERVES 6

PIQUILLO PEPPERS

Piquillo peppers are traditionally grown in the northern Spanish province of Navara. The sweet peppers are roasted over wood fires before being peeled and canned or jarred. They can simply be chopped or sliced and used as you would roasted capsicum, and their compact nature make them perfect candidates for stuffing.

This may not be everyone's idea of breakfast, but it is mine. In fact, it is very high up on my list of favourites – I do love a savoury start to the day. Inspired by son-in-law eggs, the classic Thai dish of deep-fried eggs with tamarind caramel, this is great for brunch on a warm day with fragrant black tea or fresh coconut water. It works just as well at lunchtime with some steamed dumplings, or as a side dish for a more elaborate banquet. The eggs are also brilliant in Congee (page 172).

FRIED SOFT-BOILED EGGS WITH OYSTER SAUCE, THAI BASIL, CHILLI & PICKLES

6 extra-large eggs, at room temperature
oil, for deep-frying
¼ iceberg lettuce, shredded
1 handful of mixed Spiced Chinese Pickles (page 46)
3 tablespoons oyster sauce
1 handful of Thai basil leaves
1 handful of coriander leaves
1 handful of dill fronds
3 spring onions, finely sliced
2 long red chillies, sliced
½ teaspoon sesame oil
3 teaspoons Sichuan & Mandarin Salt (page 24)

Carefully lower the eggs into a saucepan of simmering water and cook for 4½ minutes. Lift from the water and immediately refresh under cold water for 5 minutes before peeling.

Preheat a deep-fryer or saucepan of oil to 190°C.

Arrange the lettuce and pickles on a serving platter.

Deep-fry the eggs for about 2 minutes until lightly golden. Drain off a little oil and add to a bowl with the oyster sauce. Roll the eggs through the sauce to coat and place on the platter.

Add the herbs, spring onion, chilli and sesame oil to the bowl with the residual oyster sauce, toss to coat and scatter over the eggs. Slice open some of the eggs – only do this on the platter or you'll lose the yolk – and sprinkle over the Sichuan salt. Serve immediately.

SERVES 4

BREAD & CRACKERS

HOMEMADE IS BETTER

———

FLAXSEED CRACKERS

OATCAKES

BAO

NAAN

SIMIT

BRIOCHE

SUPER SEED LOAF

———

*These crackers are pretty addictive by themselves, but they're especially good with a smear of goat's curd, or some beef or tuna tartare. Crumble them over roasted vegetables (try my **Roasted Beetroot & Pumpkin Salad** on page 112), toss through a cold noodle salad or just smear with **Hummus** (page 98).*

FLAXSEED CRACKERS

500 g flaxseeds
70 ml tamari
100 g sesame seeds
100 g pumpkin seeds
1½ tablespoons fennel seeds
1 teaspoon celery seeds
2 teaspoons chilli flakes
1 teaspoon curry powder
1 teaspoon salt flakes
freshly ground black pepper

This recipe will need to be started the day before serving.

Add the flaxseeds and tamari to a large bowl and add enough water to cover by about 3 cm. Set aside for 24 hours.

Preheat the oven to 110°C fan-forced (130°C conventional). Line a baking tray with baking paper.

The flaxseeds will have swollen and become slightly gel-like overnight. Fold in the sesame seeds, pumpkin seeds, fennel seeds, celery seeds, chilli flakes, curry powder and salt and grind in plenty of pepper. Spread the mix out on the prepared tray and smooth out thinly. Bake for 3 hours, carefully flipping and peeling off the baking paper three-quarters of the way through the cooking time. Set aside to cool.

Break the cooled sheet into shards and store in an airtight container. The crackers will keep for around 2 weeks.

MAKES 600 G

FLAXSEEDS

Flaxseeds are a very good plant source of omega-3 fatty acids and are full of fibre. Flaxseeds are seen as being beneficial to heart health, and may help to lower blood pressure and bad cholesterol levels. All that omega-3 isn't hugely stable, though, and the oils can become rancid quite quickly, so make sure you obtain fresh stock and store the seeds in an airtight container somewhere cool. To get the full spectrum of their benefits, flaxseeds really need to be ground, but not all food has to be treated as medicine and their texture really makes these crackers sing.

*These oatcakes are based on the classic Scottish biscuit, and are perfect with sharp cheddar and a little **Red Onion & Sherry Jam** (page 32), **Roasted Pears with Gorgonzola** (page 251) or with some chevre and fresh figs.*

OATCAKES

120 g rolled oats
300 g plain flour
1½ tablespoons raw sugar
2 teaspoons baking powder
2 teaspoons salt flakes, plus extra
½ teaspoon freshly ground black pepper
150 g unsalted butter, softened
3–5 tablespoons milk

Preheat the oven to 160°C fan-forced (180°C conventional). Line a baking tray with baking paper.

Add 90 g of oats, the flour, sugar, baking powder, salt and pepper to a food processor and blitz for 5 seconds. Add the butter and blitz to a crumb consistency. Add 3 tablespoons of milk and process to combine. Squeeze the mix between your fingers and if it doesn't bind, add a little more milk.

Tip the crumb onto the bench and knead to bring the dough together. Press flat between two sheets of baking paper and refrigerate for 20 minutes.

Roll the rested dough to about 5-mm thick, peel off the top layer of baking paper and cut out the oatcakes with a biscuit cutter, or slice into squares or rectangles. Combine the scraps and roll again to use all the dough. Transfer to the prepared tray, sprinkle with the remaining oats and a little extra salt and bake for about 15 minutes until lightly golden. Set aside to cool.

The oatcakes will keep for about 10 days in an airtight container.

MAKES 15–20

*Bao are steamed buns popular in Chinese cuisine, and making your own for sticky **Spiced Pork Belly Bao** (page 137) or an elaborate **Bo Ssam** feast (pages 232–3) adds maximum wow to an already impressive meal. These light and airy bao are actually pretty simple to make, and if the batch isn't devoured in one sitting – and I'll be surprised if it isn't – then they freeze well too.*

BAO

14 g (2 sachets) dried yeast
80 g caster sugar
3 tablespoons melted duck or pork fat (or peanut oil), plus extra
600 g plain flour
½ teaspoon baking powder
½ teaspoon bicarbonate of soda
2 teaspoons salt flakes
1 tablespoon peanut oil
2–3 drops of sesame oil

Cut out thirty-five 10-cm squares of baking paper.

Add the yeast, sugar and 350 ml of warm water (about body temperature) to a medium bowl and whisk until combined. Set aside for a few minutes to activate the yeast before whisking in the fat.

Add the flour, baking powder and bicarbonate of soda to the bowl of a stand mixer and start mixing slowly with the dough hook. Add the yeast mix and as soon as a dough has formed, add the salt and mix briefly until smooth.

Remove the dough from the mixer and knead on the bench for 2–3 minutes until smooth and elastic. Return to the mixing bowl, cover and set aside in a warm place until doubled in size, about 40 minutes.

Combine the peanut and sesame oils in a small bowl.

Divide the dough into 30 g portions, or larger if you like, and roll into balls, lining the balls up in the order rolled. Once all have been formed, flatten out the first ball into a 10-cm long oval. Dip a finger in the oil mix and lightly brush one half of the oval. Fold the other half over to form a half-moon and place in the middle of one of the squares of baking paper. Repeat for the remaining dough. Dampen a clean Chux or lightly woven cloth with water and lightly brush the top of each bun. Cover with a damp, lightly woven tea towel and set aside somewhere warm to prove and increase in volume by half again, about 20–30 minutes.

Once rested, bring 10 cm of water to a simmer in a wok or large saucepan. Place a steamer on top and add a batch of the buns, lifting them in by the paper and being careful to leave enough space for the steam to circulate. Steam for about 12 minutes until puffed and springy to the touch. Ideally, take the steamer straight to the table to serve. You can also refrigerate or freeze at this point and simply steam again for 5 minutes to warm through. They will keep for about 5 days in the refrigerator.

MAKES ABOUT 35

*This delicious Indian flatbread is really quite easy to make at home. The yoghurt in this dough adds an appealing sour tang and keeps the bread nice and short – a perfect vehicle for a rich and spicy curry (try my Kashmiri **Rogan Josh** on page 191). You can also cook these on the flat grill of the barbecue, which makes it easy to cook them all at once or in larger batches. These also reheat well, just wrap in baking paper and foil, seal tightly and reheat in the oven.*

NAAN

150 ml milk
1½ teaspoons caster sugar
10 g (1½ sachets) dried yeast
150 g natural yoghurt
60 g butter, melted
450 g plain flour
1½ teaspoons salt

Add the milk and 150 ml of water to a small saucepan and warm to roughly body temperature. Take off the heat and whisk in the sugar and yeast. Once the mix starts to foam, whisk in the yoghurt and butter until combined.

Add the flour and salt to a large bowl and gradually mix in the liquid until you have a soft and pliable dough. Tip out onto a lightly floured bench and knead for 5 minutes. Add back to the bowl, cover and rest somewhere warm until doubled in size, about 30 minutes.

Divide the risen dough into twelve portions and roll or stretch into teardrop shapes about 5-mm thick.

Heat a large heavy-based frying pan – a cast-iron skillet is perfect – until extremely hot. Add one of the stretched pieces of dough, it will puff up immediately, and cook for 2 minutes. Flip, it should be a little scorched, and cook on the other side for 2–3 minutes. Wrap the naan in baking paper and foil to keep warm, and repeat for the remaining dough.

MAKES 12

YOGHURT

Unfortunately, the yoghurt section of most supermarkets feels more like a dessert section, with so many products loaded with thickeners, stabilisers and sugar. Yoghurt should really just be made from whole milk and live cultures. Quality natural yoghurt is a delicious wholefood that has excellent probiotic properties and countless applications in the kitchen, adding a creamy richness coupled with a balancing sour tang to all manner of dishes.

*On a food-focused trip to Istanbul, I started pretty much every day with a glass of freshly squeezed pomegranate juice and one of these freshly baked sesame-encrusted simits. I love the intense nutty sesame flavour and subtle sweetness from the grape molasses. These are amazing still warm from the oven, and best on the day that they're baked. Try them with **Hummus** (page 98), **Turkish-style Roasted Pumpkin & Walnut Dip** (page 100), a spread of mezze or just on their own.*

SIMIT

7 g (1 sachet) dried yeast
2 teaspoons caster sugar
2½ tablespoons thickened cream
1 tablespoon extra-virgin olive oil
475 g plain flour
2 teaspoons salt
100 ml grape molasses
150 g sesame seeds

Add the yeast, sugar and 375 ml of warm water (about body temperature) to a medium bowl and stir to combine. Set aside for a few minutes until the yeast is activated and the mix starts to foam. Add the cream and oil and combine.

Add the flour and salt to the bowl of a stand mixer and start mixing on slow using the dough hook. Gradually add the liquid until incorporated, and mix until a smooth dough forms. Cover and set aside somewhere warm until doubled in size, about 40 minutes.

Preheat the oven to 230°C fan-forced (250°C conventional). Line two baking trays with baking paper.

Tip the rested dough out of the bowl and divide into ten evenly sized balls. Set aside to rest for 5 minutes.

Cut a rested dough ball in half and roll with your hands into two strips about 30-cm long. Twist the strips together into a rope and press both ends together to form a circle. Repeat for all the dough.

Combine the grape molasses, 100 ml of water and a couple of pinches of salt in a shallow bowl. Add the sesame seeds to another shallow bowl.

Dip each ring in the diluted molasses, gently shaking off any excess before adding to the sesame seeds to coat. Place on the prepared trays and bake for about 20 minutes, rotating the trays halfway through the cooking time, until golden.

MAKES 10

SIMIT

Simit has been a feature of Istanbul's streets for several hundred years, and the traditional red carts a fixture in living memory. Simit is the most emblematic street food of Istanbul and is sold everywhere, from modern chain stores to simple street vendors with trays balanced on their heads. They are baked throughout the day and eaten as fresh as possible, but the subtle sweetness from the grape molasses makes them particularly enjoyable in the morning. They are made in other parts of Turkey, and a very similar bread, koulouri, is also made in Greece, especially in Thessaloniki.

*Brioche is such a classic old-fashioned French bread, laden with as much butter and egg as it can carry, and perhaps as a consequence it fell out of fashion for a little while. It's certainly made a strong comeback of late, becoming almost the essential burger bun, and, although often softer and lighter than is traditional, as the buttery shell of a lobster roll. Brioche is delicious toasted and served with terrine or pâté (try my **Chicken Liver Parfait** on pages 202–3), with herb-flecked scrambled eggs or gently melted Comté cheese and sautéed mushrooms, or turned into a decadent bread and butter pudding. And if you want that lobster roll experience at home, try my **Brioche Rolls with Crayfish** (page 140).*

BRIOCHE

25 g (1½ tablespoons) caster sugar, plus 1 pinch extra
260 g unsalted butter, softened
14 g (2 sachets) dried yeast
2½ tablespoons milk
5 × 55 g eggs, at room temperature
450 g plain flour
10 g (1¼ teaspoons) salt
1 tablespoon sesame seeds

This recipe will need to be started the day before serving.

Add 25 g of sugar and the butter to the bowl of a stand mixer and beat with the paddle attachment until pale and creamy, about 2 minutes. Remove from the bowl and set aside.

Add the yeast, milk and a pinch of sugar to a medium bowl and whisk to combine. Add four eggs, keeping one aside to glaze the rolls, and whisk until combined.

Sift the flour and salt into the bowl of the stand mixer. Pour in the milk and egg mix while mixing on medium with the dough hook. Continue mixing for 8–10 minutes until smooth – you may need to scrape the dough down the hook every now and then. Once the dough is a smooth mass on the end of the hook, add about 2 tablespoons of the creamed butter while mixing. Keep adding the butter in batches until well incorporated. Continue to mix for about 5 minutes until the dough is shiny and elastic. Place the dough in a large greased bowl, cover with plastic wrap and set aside until it has doubled in size, about 2 hours. The room temperature will naturally alter the required proving time, just don't get it too warm or the butter will melt out of the dough.

Knock back the rested dough with your fist, cover and refrigerate overnight.

The next day, tip the dough onto a lightly floured surface – it should now be firm but quite malleable – and divide into twelve 80 g portions. Shape the dough into buns by rolling under your palm in a circular action until even and smooth. Flip one bun over and flatten out a little into an elongated oval. Roll one edge in towards the middle and press the seam together along the length of the

roll where it meets the other edge. Flip so that the seam is on the bottom and place on a lined baking tray. Repeat for all the dough, spacing out the rolls evenly on the tray. Cover the shaped dough with a damp, lightweight tea towel and set aside until doubled in size, about 2–3 hours.

Preheat the oven to 200°C fan-forced (220°C conventional).

Beat the remaining egg and glaze the top of the proved rolls. Sprinkle over the sesame seeds and bake for about 16 minutes until a deeply golden caramel – cooking time will naturally vary depending on the oven, so watch carefully. Cool on a wire rack before using.

MAKES 12 ROLLS

*This is a densely packed, gluten-free loaf full of superfood punch. If the notion of superfoods doesn't particularly ring your bell, it's also just plain delicious. I like this on its own when it's just freshly baked, but it's also great with **Hummus** (page 98), butter and jam (try my **Simple Roasted Raspberry Jam** on page 14), or goat's curd. Store in a sealed container for a couple of days, or refrigerate for a slightly longer shelf life.*

SUPER SEED LOAF

150 g white quinoa, rinsed
100 g pure maple syrup
3 tablespoons coconut oil
2 teaspoons caraway seeds
2 teaspoons fennel seeds
20 grinds of black pepper
3 teaspoons salt flakes
150 g raw almonds
100 g flaxseeds
150 g sunflower seeds
35 g chia seeds
80 g pumpkin seeds
30 g psyllium husk powder
35 g sesame seeds
40 g coconut flour
1 tablespoon maca powder

TO LINE THE TIN
2 tablespoons sesame seeds
2 tablespoons pumpkin seeds
1 tablespoon fennel seeds

Add the quinoa to a saucepan of boiling water and cook until tender, about 8–10 minutes. Drain well.

Combine the maple syrup, coconut oil, caraway and fennel seeds, pepper, salt and 650 ml of water in a medium saucepan and warm gently over low heat to combine.

Add the almonds, flaxseeds, sunflower seeds and chia seeds to a food processor and blitz to a fine powder.

Add the almond and seed mix to a large bowl with the quinoa, pumpkin seeds, psyllium powder, sesame seeds, coconut flour and maca powder and combine. Pour in the liquid mix and combine, adding a splash more water if needed to bring the mix together – the dough should still be quite thick.

Grease two 23–25-cm loaf tins, line with baking paper and then grease the paper. Line the tins with most of the sesame seeds, pumpkin seeds and fennel seeds, leaving some aside to top the loaves. Divide the dough between the tins, packing it in firmly, top with the remaining seeds and set aside at room temperature for 2 hours.

Preheat the oven to 180°C fan-forced (200°C conventional).

Bake the loaves for 50 minutes before unmoulding and placing back in the oven on a baking tray for 5–10 minutes to brown – this last step isn't essential, but it does lift the presentation. Set aside to cool before slicing.

MAKES 2 LOAVES

COLD, LIGHT, LEAFY & RAW

EAT WELL AND FEEL GOOD

———

HUMMUS WITH SPICED CHICKPEAS & HONEYED YOGHURT

TURKISH-STYLE ROASTED PUMPKIN & WALNUT DIP

SUPER GREEN SALAD WITH SHIITAKE & GINGER

RAW SLAW WITH TOFU & PEANUT MAYONNAISE

EGG, EGGPLANT & OLIVE SALAD WITH SESAME, MINT & DUKKAH

ORANGE-GLAZED SWEET POTATO WITH FENNEL & PITA

ROASTED BEETROOT & PUMPKIN SALAD WITH GOAT'S CURD & SEED CRACKERS

CURED OCEAN TROUT WITH WONTON CRACKERS, SICHUAN SALT & SESAME MAYONNAISE

ROASTED OCEAN TROUT WITH TABOULI-STYLE SALAD & POMEGRANATE MOLASSES

SASHIMI TUNA WITH AVOCADO, WASABI PEAS & GINGER DRESSING

———

Making your own hummus is particularly satisfying, and so simple. There are a couple of tricks, though, that help to make it really special. Cooking the chickpeas with a little bicarbonate of soda softens the skins, making for a silken texture, and the addition of iced water while processing helps to make it extra light and fluffy.

*The quantities of both lemon juice and garlic can be seen as more of a guide, simply adjust to your taste. And the fried and spiced chickpeas are very much an optional garnish, but they do add a personal touch and elevate the dish into quite a pretty starter. Add a little fried haloumi, some pickled turnip, a bowl of good olives and pide or homemade **Simit** (page 88) and you've got a great start to a meal. I also love hummus with fried eggs, spread on **Flaxseed Crackers** (page 78) or **Super Seed Loaf** (page 94), or served with fried fish.*

HUMMUS WITH SPICED CHICKPEAS & HONEYED YOGHURT

2 tablespoons extra-virgin olive oil

1 × 400 g can chickpeas, drained, rinsed thoroughly and drained again

2 teaspoons ground cumin

½ teaspoon ground allspice

salt flakes and freshly ground black pepper

100 g natural yoghurt

1 tablespoon honey

½ lemon

1 handful of flat-leaf parsley leaves

pide or Simit (page 88), to serve

HUMMUS

200 g dried chickpeas, soaked overnight in plenty of water

1½ teaspoons bicarbonate of soda

180 g tahini

2 garlic cloves, finely grated

100 ml lemon juice

salt flakes

150 ml ice-cold water

For the hummus, drain the chickpeas and place in a large saucepan with the bicarbonate of soda and enough water to just cover. Place over high heat, bring to the boil and cook for 5 minutes, stirring occasionally. Add 1.5 litres of water and bring to a simmer. Skim and cook for 45 minutes to an hour until the chickpeas are tender enough to crush easily under thumb. Drain very well.

Add the cooked chickpeas to a food processor and blitz to a stiff paste. Add the tahini, garlic, lemon juice and 1 tablespoon of salt flakes and process until combined. Drizzle in the iced water while processing until the hummus is light and fluffy. Adjust the seasoning if necessary.

For the garnish, add the oil and canned chickpeas to a large frying pan and place over medium heat – if you add the chickpeas to hot oil they will spit and can be quite hazardous – and fry until golden. Tip out of the pan into a medium bowl, scatter over the spices, season and toss to coat.

Combine the yoghurt and honey in a small bowl and squeeze in lemon juice to taste.

Smear the hummus on a serving plate, spoon over the yoghurt sauce, top with the spiced chickpeas and parsley and serve with fresh pide or simit.

MAKES ABOUT 3 CUPS

Pumpkin is famously used in Turkey to make kabak tatlisi, *a candied pumpkin dish that is one of the country's most well-loved desserts. In fact, it is pretty hard to find any references to savoury applications in Turkish cookbooks, but on an all too brief food pilgrimage to Istanbul I actually came across many versions of pumpkin dip. Whether traditional or not, pumpkin's sweet richness coupled with the classic flavours of tahini, walnuts, lemon juice and pomegranate molasses makes for a delicious savoury treat. This works beautifully as part of a feast, and if you make your own* **Simit** *(page 88), it presents as an elegant dish all on its own. It's also great spread on toast and topped with a poached egg for breakfast.*

TURKISH-STYLE ROASTED PUMPKIN & WALNUT DIP

1 small white onion, sliced into rings

extra-virgin olive oil

freshly ground black pepper

1½ tablespoons black tahini

50 g walnuts, toasted and tossed in extra-virgin olive oil and salt while hot, roughly smashed

1 handful of coriander leaves (optional)

½ lemon

Simit (page 88) or pide, to serve

PUMPKIN DIP

1 kg Kent pumpkin, skin on, cut into large chunks

1 teaspoon ground cinnamon

1 teaspoon ground allspice

100 g walnuts, roasted

2½ tablespoons extra-virgin olive oil, plus extra

3 tablespoons tahini

3 tablespoons pomegranate molasses

finely grated zest of ½ lemon

juice of 1 lemon

3 teaspoons salt flakes

Preheat the oven to 180°C fan-forced (200°C conventional). Line a baking tray with baking paper.

Add the pumpkin to a large bowl, scatter over the cinnamon and allspice and toss until evenly coated. Spread the pumpkin out on the prepared tray and dry roast for about 1 hour until tender. Set aside to cool.

Soak the onion in a bowl of cold water for 10 minutes. Drain and pat dry with paper towel. Add to a small bowl and toss with a little oil and pepper.

For the dip, add the walnuts to a blender and process until quite fine. Gradually add 2 tablespoons of water followed by the oil to form a paste. Scoop the pumpkin flesh from the skin and add to the blender along with the tahini, pomegranate molasses, lemon zest and juice and salt. Blend until smooth, scraping down the side of the jug to combine evenly.

Spoon the dip onto a lipped plate, drizzle over the black tahini, scatter over the onion, smashed walnuts and coriander (if using) and squeeze over some lemon juice. Serve with the simit or pide.

SERVES 4–6

Leeks make a big contribution to so many dishes, but they tend to do so in the shadows, cooked down, blitzed or used for flavour and discarded. They deserve a bit more of the limelight. They work brilliantly in this salad, adding distinctive flavour and a textural foil to the chewy kale, smooth avocado, earthy shiitake and crunchy, peppery wasabi crumb. This healthful salad is delicious by itself, but it would also make a perfect partner to a steak marinated in kecap manis (Indonesian sweet soy sauce) and seared on a hot grill, or with some simply poached chicken.

SUPER GREEN SALAD WITH SHIITAKE & GINGER

10 shiitake mushrooms, stems trimmed

1 leek, white and pale green parts only, trimmed

150 g kale leaves

250 g baby spinach leaves

150 g bean sprouts

2 tablespoons mirin

2 ripe avocados, sliced

5 spring onions, white part only, finely sliced

2 handfuls of wasabi peas, crushed using a mortar and pestle

2 sheets of toasted nori

GINGER & SOY DRESSING

10-cm piece of ginger, finely grated

2 tablespoons grapeseed oil (or other neutral oil)

2 tablespoons soy sauce

1½ tablespoons mirin

1 tablespoon lemon juice

2 teaspoons umeboshi puree

1 teaspoon sesame oil

For the dressing, combine all the ingredients in a small bowl.

Cook the shiitakes in simmering salted water for 5 minutes, drain, toss with a little dressing and set aside.

Cook the leek in simmering salted water for 10 minutes, refresh under cold water and drain. Wrap the leek in paper towel and gently squeeze out any excess liquid. Slice into 2-cm rounds.

Blanch the kale in boiling salted water for 2 minutes. Lift out of the water, refresh under cold water, drain and squeeze out any excess moisture. Repeat for the spinach but only blanch for 1 minute. Blanch the bean sprouts for 30 seconds, refresh and drain well.

Dress the bean sprouts with the mirin and arrange on a serving platter.

Add the spinach and kale to a medium bowl and dress with a little of the dressing. Toss and arrange on top of the bean sprouts. Follow with the avocado, leek, spring onion and shiitakes. Scatter over the wasabi pea powder and spoon over the remaining dressing. Fold up the nori sheets and snip finely with scissors over the salad and serve.

SERVES 4–6

KALE

Kale has become so popular that it's as easy to find at the supermarket as lettuce. I must say that I've come to really appreciate both its flavour and distinctive textural chew. It's great blanched and used in salads, and goes especially well with the soft richness of roasted pumpkin. You can also dehydrate the leaves in a low oven for a healthy snacking chip or use them to add crunch to a salad. Kale is a bit of a sponge and will really soak up sauces, taking up flavour as it cooks, and it's surprisingly good in Chinese-inspired dishes. Some mornings, especially if it's cold, I'll shred some kale leaves and cook them down in a little broth to have with a fried egg and a good wedge of avocado.

The benefits of eating kale are pretty hard to go past – it is high in fibre and an incredibly rich source of vitamins A, K and C – but you can overdo it. Raw kale shakes have become fashionable amongst the health conscious, but along with the great benefits comes a downside. Kale contains a decent amount of oxalic acid – the thing that makes rhubarb leaves so toxic – which is not a problem in moderation and is usually offset by the benefits. But if you're taking the more is better approach with raw kale, you might run into some problems. Oxalic acid is essentially toxic, protecting plants from predators, with symptoms ranging from digestive discomfort to death. Oxalic acid also tends to crystallise in the human system and can negatively impact health, especially if you're prone to kidney stones. It can also disrupt normal thyroid function. Cooking kale will significantly reduce the impact of both issues, and more so if you drain off the water. You'll lose some of the good stuff, but blanching kale before using will not only make it a bit easier to eat, it'll also knock out some of the negatives.

I love the crunchy sweetness of raw beetroot, and, if you haven't tried it before, raw kohlrabi is a bit of a revelation. They both work particularly well with this egg-free mayonnaise that is given earthy weight by the peanut butter and a subtle tweak of sourness from the umeboshi. This salad is particularly good in the cooler months when cabbage is at its sweet best, and can be taken a step further by adding a handful of shredded shiso, Thai basil, coriander or mint.

The key to this salad is shaving the vegetables very finely, so unless you particularly like to show off your knife skills, use a mandoline. Every domestic kitchen should have one, pretty much every commercial kitchen does. Combine and dress this salad just before serving, otherwise the beetroot will bleed and affect the presentation.

RAW SLAW WITH TOFU & PEANUT MAYONNAISE

4 striped baby beetroots

¼ white cabbage, finely shaved

1 kohlrabi, peeled, cut in half and finely shaved

2 carrots, finely sliced

5 spring onions, white part only, finely sliced

2 long red chillies, finely sliced

salt flakes

1 tablespoon poppy seeds

2 tablespoons chopped roasted peanuts

TOFU & PEANUT MAYONNAISE

200 g silken tofu

80 ml grapeseed oil (or other neutral oil)

3 tablespoons honey

2 tablespoons apple cider vinegar

2 heaped tablespoons salted smooth peanut butter

1 tablespoon umeboshi puree

1 tablespoon Dijon mustard

2 teaspoons miso paste

For the tofu mayonnaise, add all the ingredients to a blender or food processor and process until smooth.

Trim the beetroots, leaving 2–3 cm of stalk attached. Scrub and wash well, being sure to dislodge any dirt trapped in the stalks. Finely slice lengthways on a mandoline and add to a large bowl with the cabbage, kohlrabi, carrot, spring onion and chilli. Season with salt, scatter on the poppy seeds, tip over the dressing and toss to combine.

Pile the salad into a serving bowl, scatter over the peanuts and serve immediately.

SERVES 6–8

UMEBOSHI

Umeboshi are salted and pickled Japanese plums. Well, the ume fruit are not actually plums as such, but rather have genetic links to both plums and apricots. Traditionally, their uses were medicinal rather than culinary, but today they very much take their place on the table. I love the salty and sour qualities of umeboshi, and I often use the puree to tweak dressings and sauces.

This is an unusual salad that was inspired by one of Greg Malouf's brilliant dishes. There's something about the rich eggs and soft eggplant combined with the spices, olives, pine nuts and sesame that I find incredibly luxurious. Serve it on its own or with spiced grilled chicken or beef. As an optional garnish, shred some of the eggplant skin and shallow-fry until crisp.

EGG, EGGPLANT & OLIVE SALAD WITH SESAME, MINT & DUKKAH

1 large eggplant, peeled and cut into 2-cm dice

juice of ½ lemon

4 eggs, at room temperature

100 g pine nuts, lightly toasted

50 g manzanilla olives, pitted and roughly chopped

1 tablespoon toasted sesame seeds

½ red onion, finely sliced

1 long green chilli, deseeded and finely sliced

½ small garlic clove, very finely chopped

2 teaspoons sumac

1 teaspoon chilli powder

2 tablespoons extra-virgin olive oil

salt flakes

1 tablespoon Dukkah (page 27)

6 mint sprigs, leaves picked

6 radishes, with some stalk and leaf still attached, halved

fresh pide, to serve

TAHINI DRESSING

2 tablespoons tahini

2 tablespoons lemon juice

1 tablespoon water

salt flakes and freshly ground black pepper

Add the eggplant and lemon juice to a large saucepan of boiling salted water and cook for about 10 minutes until tender. Drain the eggplant and dry well on paper towel.

Add the eggs to a saucepan of boiling water and simmer for 6 minutes. Immediately plunge into cold water and peel once cool.

For the dressing, add all the ingredients to a small jar and season to taste. Seal with the lid and shake vigorously to combine.

Slice the eggs in half and then into large dice. Add to a large bowl with the eggplant, pine nuts, olives, sesame seeds, onion, green chilli, garlic, sumac, chilli powder, oil and a pinch of salt and combine gently.

Pile the salad into a bowl and carefully tip out in a mound onto a serving platter. Spoon the dressing over the top, scatter over the dukkah, mint and radish and serve with the pide.

SERVES 4

TAHINI

Throw out that old jar of tahini lurking in the fridge and start fresh. Like the oil from any seed or nut, sesame oil will become rancid over time. It also tends to become more bitter the older it gets, and that dish you've gone to the trouble of making will be ruined in an instant.

I eat fennel, orange and olive salad a lot at home, especially in winter when fennel and Australian navel oranges are at their best. This version casts sweet potato as the unlikely hero, with the orange glaze giving it an intense caramel note and a spike of acidity. I like to keep the bread nice and crisp as a textural contrast, but, if you prefer, you can leave it in the dressing until softened. This is perfect with roast pork, grilled blue-eye trevalla or other meaty white fish, or spiced roast chicken. Or make this into a meal by itself by adding a jar or can of quality tuna in oil.

ORANGE-GLAZED SWEET POTATO WITH FENNEL & PITA

3 small sweet potatoes, cut lengthways into 2-cm thick slices

3 small white pita rounds, split open

1 teaspoon cumin seeds, roughly ground

2½ tablespoons extra-virgin olive oil

2 tablespoons Mayonnaise (for a recipe, see page 31)

1 tablespoon natural yoghurt

1 large lemon

2 long green chillies, finely sliced

finely grated zest and juice of 1 orange

1 large fennel bulb, finely sliced, fronds reserved

12 kalamata olives, pitted

ORANGE GLAZE

juice of 3 oranges

1½ teaspoons fennel seeds, roughly smashed

salt flakes and freshly ground black pepper

1½ tablespoons extra-virgin olive oil

Preheat the oven to 160°C fan-forced (180°C conventional). Line a baking tray with baking paper.

For the glaze, add the orange juice and fennel seeds to a small saucepan over medium heat and reduce the liquid by half. Take off the heat, season and add the oil.

Add the sweet potato to a large bowl, pour over the glaze and toss to coat. Spread the sweet potato out on the prepared tray, tipping over any liquid in the bowl, and roast for 40 minutes. Set aside to cool before cutting the slices in half lengthways.

Place the split pitas on a baking tray, sprinkle over the cumin, season and drizzle with ½ tablespoon of oil. Bake for 10–15 minutes until crisp and lightly golden. Set aside to cool – the pitas will crisp up more as they cool.

Add the mayonnaise, yoghurt and a small squeeze of lemon juice to a small bowl and combine.

Add the chilli, orange zest and juice and remaining 2 tablespoons of oil to a large bowl, squeeze in the rest of the lemon, season and combine. Add the fennel and olives and break in the bread in large shards. Toss through gently.

Smear the mayonnaise mix across a serving plate, top with the sweet potato, pile on the salad, scatter over the fennel fronds and serve.

SERVES 6

*This chunky roasted vegetable salad is a perfect lunch on its own, or would make a great partner to a grilled steak or roast chicken. It also presents beautifully and is an easy way to make a good impression if you're asked to bring a plate. If you don't have the **Flaxseed Crackers** (page 78) in the pantry, try crumbled pumpernickel, or toasted walnuts or almonds. Also, if preferred, thick natural yoghurt, labna or fried haloumi would make good replacements for the goat's curd.*

ROASTED BEETROOT & PUMPKIN SALAD WITH GOAT'S CURD & SEED CRACKERS

¼ small Kent pumpkin, skin on, cut into 5 wedges

3 beetroots, trimmed, scrubbed and sliced into 1.5-cm thick discs

salt flakes and freshly ground black pepper

1 teaspoon ground cinnamon

extra-virgin olive oil

3 heaped tablespoons goat's curd

2 handfuls broken Flaxseed Crackers (page 78)

1 handful of dill fronds

HONEY & CHILLI DRESSING

80 ml extra-virgin olive oil

3 tablespoons honey (or pure maple syrup)

2 tablespoons apple cider vinegar

2 long red chillies

½ teaspoon salt flakes

1 handful of dill fronds, chopped

Preheat the oven to 180°C fan-forced (200°C conventional). Line two baking trays with baking paper.

Place the pumpkin and beetroot on separate prepared trays, season, sprinkle over the cinnamon and drizzle over a little oil. Roast until tender – about 40 minutes for the beetroot, and about 50 minutes for the pumpkin. Cut the pumpkin wedges in half again and set aside with the beetroot to cool.

For the dressing, combine all the ingredients in a small bowl.

Arrange the pumpkin and beetroot on a serving plate, dollop on the goat's curd, scatter over the crackers and dill, spoon over the dressing and serve.

SERVES 6

PUMPKIN

My all-round pumpkin of choice is the Kent pumpkin. They have such sweetly rich flesh and they're great for roasting, which is something I tend to do no matter what dish they're intended for. Even if you're using pumpkin in a soup, curry or stew, roasting it first will concentrate the flavour and texture and add deeper caramelised notes to the finished dish. Try sprinkling pumpkin with some spices before roasting: cumin, cinnamon, black pepper and spice mixes like ras el hanout or baharat are perfect. Dressing the cooked flesh with a little vinegar adds a nice foil to the richness, and it also gives it a real zing when served cold. Cold roasted pumpkin is great in a couscous or grain salad.

I'm a big fan of cured ocean trout and usually pair it with traditional flavours, such as dill, red onion, crème fraîche and the like, but the rich flesh of the trout is also great matched with Sichuan pepper, dried mandarin, spring onions and pickled ginger. Add to this the crunch of crisp fried wonton skins and a toasty sesame mayonnaise and you've got some seriously great finger food – perfect with cold beer or Champagne. This dish can be presented as a platter of components, allowing your guests to make up their own, or you can make up individual canapés to pass around.

CURED OCEAN TROUT WITH WONTON CRACKERS, SICHUAN SALT & SESAME MAYONNAISE

100 g pickled ginger, finely sliced, pickling liquid reserved

6 spring onions, very finely sliced

grapeseed oil (or other neutral oil), for shallow-frying

25 large square wonton wrappers, cut into triangles

½ quantity Sichuan & Mandarin Salt (page 24)

1 side of Citrus-cured Ocean Trout (page 51)

5 kaffir lime leaves, very finely sliced

1 celery heart, leaves only

SESAME MAYONNAISE

250 g Mayonnaise (for a recipe, see page 31)

50 g sesame seeds, toasted and ground

2 teaspoons sesame oil

2 tablespoons rice wine vinegar

For the sesame mayonnaise, combine all the ingredients in a bowl and scoop into a piping bag fitted with a fine nozzle. Refrigerate until needed.

Add the ginger and spring onion to a small bowl and dress with a little ginger pickling liquid and 2 teaspoons of grapeseed oil.

Heat 2–3 cm of grapeseed oil in a deep-sided frying pan or saucepan until 180°C and fry the wonton wrappers until lightly golden. Drain on paper towel and season with a little Sichuan salt while still hot.

Slice the fish thinly and arrange on a serving platter. Pipe dots of mayonnaise onto each piece of fish and scatter over the lime leaves and celery leaves. Pile the fried wontons next to the fish and serve with the pickled ginger and spring onion mix and remaining Sichuan salt on the side.

SERVES 10–12

SICHUAN PEPPERCORNS

Sichuan peppercorns are as important to Sichuan cuisine as chillies, and that's really saying something. They're not related to black peppercorns, and the aroma is distinctly individual with floral tea-like characteristics and, for me, a hint of dried wild mint. The first time I had any real contact with them was during a cooking demonstration that I did with Kylie Kwong. We were both cooking mussels, I think, and in very different ways. I really found the aroma of the toasting peppercorns quite captivating and since then I've also fallen in love with their unusual numbing effect, finding it somewhat addictive. Sichuan pepper works especially well with rich proteins like duck and pork.

This dish evolved out of playing with variations of tabouli and is perfect for lunch or a light dinner on a hot day. The flavours and textures work so well with the roasted trout, especially when combined with subtle notes of cinnamon, sumac and cumin and the tartly sweet spike of pomegranate molasses.

This method of cooking the fish yields a beautifully moist and delicate result, but it's important to follow the steps properly. If the tray isn't hot when the trout goes in the oven it will take a lot longer for the parcel to heat up. And if you open the foil too early, you will lose all the heat and steam and the fish won't finish cooking properly.

ROASTED OCEAN TROUT WITH TABOULI-STYLE SALAD & POMEGRANATE MOLASSES

1 x 600 g mid-loin ocean trout fillet, skin removed and discarded

2 teaspoons ground cumin

salt flakes and freshly ground black pepper

150 g fine cracked wheat

1 teaspoon ground cinnamon

extra-virgin olive oil

1 red onion, finely sliced into rounds

juice of ½ lemon

1 garlic clove, finely grated

2 handfuls of flat-leaf parsley leaves, chopped

2 handfuls of mint leaves, chopped

1 handful of watercress, picked

2 Lebanese cucumbers, deseeded and finely sliced

2 teaspoons sumac

3 tablespoons pomegranate molasses

Preheat the oven to 200°C fan-forced (220°C conventional). Preheat a baking tray in the oven.

Lay out a sheet of foil on the bench and top with a sheet of baking paper. Place the trout on the baking paper, sprinkle over the cumin, season and wrap into a sealed parcel. Place on the preheated baking tray and roast for 12 minutes. Set aside for 8–10 minutes before opening the foil – the fish will finish cooking in the residual heat and steam. Once opened, set aside to cool to room temperature, but please don't refrigerate.

Add the cracked wheat to a medium bowl. Sprinkle over the cinnamon, drizzle over a little oil, season and mix through. Just cover with boiling water, seal with plastic wrap and set aside for 20 minutes.

Add the onion to a bowl of cold water and set aside for 10 minutes.

Combine the lemon juice, garlic and 3 tablespoons of oil in a small bowl.

Fluff the cracked wheat with a fork and pour over the dressing. Add the herbs, watercress and cucumber and combine.

Drain the onion, dry with paper towel and toss with the sumac.

Break the trout into large pieces with your hands and arrange on a platter, pile the cracked wheat salad and onion on top, drizzle the pomegranate molasses mostly over the fish and serve.

SERVES 4

This is such a fresh and elegant shared dish, but decadent at the same time – perfect for entertaining. This only takes a matter of moments to present as a platter of sparkling fresh components, just leave your guests to compose their own little morsels while you get your other kitchen tasks out of the way.

SASHIMI TUNA WITH AVOCADO, WASABI PEAS & GINGER DRESSING

400 g sashimi-grade yellowfin tuna

4 spring onions, white and pale green parts only, finely sliced

100 g pickled ginger, julienned, pickling liquid reserved

2 avocados, sliced

3 tablespoons wasabi peas, crushed using a mortar and pestle

6 sheets of toasted nori, cut into large triangles

1½ tablespoons toasted sesame seeds

1 bunch of watercress, picked

5 shiso leaves, torn

GINGER DRESSING

4-cm piece of ginger, finely grated

3 tablespoons light soy sauce

1½ tablespoons lemon juice

1 tablespoon grapeseed oil (or other neutral oil)

¼ teaspoon sesame oil

For the dressing, combine all the ingredients in a small bowl or jug and set aside for 10 minutes before using.

Cut the tuna into 5-mm thick slices and arrange on a serving platter.

Add the spring onion and pickled ginger to a small serving dish, pour over a little of the ginger pickling liquid and place on the platter.

Arrange the avocado next to the tuna and sprinkle over the wasabi pea powder. Place the nori triangles in a small glass and add to the platter along with a small bowl of sesame seeds and a pile of watercress and shiso.

Serve as is, leaving your guests to do the assembling. Using the nori as a wrapper, fill with some avocado, a piece of tuna, a little watercress and some shiso. Top with the ginger and spring onion mix, some sesame seeds and a drizzle of dressing.

SERVES 4–6

SHISO

Shiso is a leafy herb that's also known as perilla – an abbreviation of the botanical name – and can be found in both green and purple-tinged versions, with the latter being used to add the distinctive colour to umeboshi (Japanese pickled plums, see page 107). The first time I ever ate it was with raw calamari, and I hunted it down in a Japanese supermarket soon after. The flavour is quite intense, and perhaps a little polarising, with a peppery herbaceous quality that is very distinctive and not really comparable to any other herb. It's great with rich and fatty raw foods like tuna or avocado, and it works beautifully alongside toasted nori. The leaves can be used to wrap up one-bite morsels, or shredded to add to salads and noodle dishes or to sprinkle over raw or quickly cured fish.

HANDS ON
LEAVE THE CUTLERY IN THE DRAWER

POPCORN WITH SHERRY VINEGAR & CHORIZO DUST

SWEET POTATO CHIPS WITH PAPRIKA AIOLI

CROQUETAS DE JAMON

**PRAWN & MUSHROOM SPRING ROLLS
WITH CHINESE PICKLES**

**EMPANADAS WITH SAUSAGE RAGU,
EGG & OLIVES**

**SPICED PORK BELLY BAO WITH SESAME
MAYONNAISE & GOCHUJANG**

**BRIOCHE ROLLS WITH CRAYFISH, KIMCHI
& SESAME MAYONNAISE**

GALATA BRIDGE SANDWICH

KOREAN-STYLE FRIED CHICKEN

**BÁNH MÌ:
CORIANDER & BLACK PEPPER TOFU
PORK BELLY
CHICKEN**

LAMB RIBS WITH MISO, CHILLI & DARK ALE

PEANUT BUTTER COOKIE ICE CREAM SANDWICHES

**DOUGHNUTS WITH CINNAMON & CLOVE SUGAR
& DULCE DE LECHE**

This is pretty sophisticated popcorn, and a bit of an update on the salt and vinegar chips that were a slightly more common snack when I was growing up. Mind you, this probably suits more of a grown up palate. This would make a great aperitivo snack with a briny fino sherry, or with a few cold beers watching the soccer or football.

POPCORN WITH SHERRY VINEGAR & CHORIZO DUST

2 tablespoons olive oil
180 g spicy cured chorizo, sliced
1 tablespoon salt flakes
200 g popcorn kernels
2 ½ tablespoons sherry vinegar

Add half the oil to a heavy, wide-based saucepan over low–medium heat. Fry the chorizo for a few minutes on each side until crisp. Remove from the pan and drain on paper towel. Set aside to cool completely.

Add the cooled chorizo and the salt to a spice grinder and blitz to a powder.

Add the remaining oil to the pan over high heat and add the popcorn kernels. Coat the kernels with oil, cover the pan and wait until all the kernels have popped.

Tip the popcorn into a serving bowl, drizzle over the sherry vinegar and scatter over half the chorizo dust. Toss well and serve with the remaining chorizo dust sprinkled over the top.

SERVES 6–8

It's not that easy to make sweet potato chips crunchy, but this simple method matches the subtle sweetness of the potato with a deliciously crunchy outer shell. These are a great little snack on their own, or pair them with roast lamb, grilled beef or chicken. Don't be tempted to omit baking the chips, as it dehydrates them enough to stop them being soggy, and they also won't cook in the brief time it takes to crisp up the batter.

SWEET POTATO CHIPS WITH PAPRIKA AIOLI

4 small sweet potatoes, skin on, scrubbed

3 tablespoons extra-virgin olive oil

salt flakes

oil, for deep-frying

2 eggwhites

150 g tapioca flour

150 g plain flour

1 tablespoon Celery & Black Pepper Salt (page 26), plus extra

PAPRIKA AIOLI

200 g Mayonnaise (for a recipe, see page 31)

1 large garlic clove, finely grated or crushed

2 pinches of mild smoked paprika

For the paprika aioli, combine all the ingredients in a small bowl.

Preheat the oven to 180°C fan-forced (200°C conventional). Line two baking trays with baking paper.

Slice the sweet potatoes into finger-thick chips and place on the prepared trays. Drizzle over the olive oil, season with salt flakes and toss gently to coat. Spread the chips out evenly and bake for 15 minutes. Set aside to cool on the trays.

Preheat a deep-fryer or saucepan of oil to 180°C.

Whisk the eggwhites with 1 tablespoon of water until loosened.

Add the tapioca flour, plain flour and 1 tablespoon of celery salt to a large bowl and dry whisk to combine and break up any clumps.

Working in batches of five, add the cooled chips to the flour mix and toss through gently to coat. Dust off any excess flour, dredge in the eggwhite and toss again in the flour. Deep-fry for about 2 minutes until crisp. Drain on paper towel and season with extra celery salt. Serve immediately, or keep warm in a low oven while you cook the remaining batches. Serve with the paprika aioli on the side.

SERVES 4

This is a classic Spanish tapas recipe that makes the most of any trimmings and leftover bits of jamon. These croquetas are deliciously decadent finger food, and make a perfect little Friday night snack with a glass of wine, sherry or cold beer. If you don't need the whole batch, just freeze the remainder – they're a handy little surprise to have up your sleeve when time is against you.

CROQUETAS DE JAMON

oil, for deep-frying
150 g plain flour
2 eggs, beaten
200 g dry breadcrumbs

CROQUETAS
30 g butter
1 leek, white and pale green
   parts only, diced
salt flakes
1 litre milk
200 g jamon, cut into
   5-mm dice
100 ml extra-virgin olive oil
125 g plain flour
½ teaspoon ground
   white pepper

To make the croquetas, melt the butter in a medium saucepan over medium heat. Add the leek and a pinch of salt and cook until softened, about 5 minutes. Remove from the heat and set aside.

Add the milk and jamon to a medium saucepan and bring to just under the boil. Strain the milk into a bowl and set it and the jamon aside.

Add the oil and flour to a medium saucepan over medium heat and stir constantly until golden. Take off the heat, add 250 ml of the warm milk and stir until smooth. Return the pan to the heat and stir continuously for 2 minutes over low–medium heat. Add the remaining milk off the heat and stir to combine. Place back over the heat and simmer, stirring continuously, until thickened. If the sauce starts to boil, take the pan off the heat for a moment to cool slightly before proceeding.

Add the jamon, leek and white pepper to the sauce off the heat, season to taste and stir until combined. Tip the mix into a tray or container and refrigerate for 3–4 hours, or preferably overnight.

Take 1 heaped tablespoon of the cooled croqueta mix, mould into a barrel in your hands and place on a lined tray in the refrigerator – this will help the croquetas hold their shape. Repeat for all the mix.

Preheat a deep-fryer or saucepan of oil to 180°C.

Roll the croquetas in the flour, then dip in the egg wash and finally coat with the breadcrumbs. The croquetas can be frozen at this stage, simply thaw in the fridge for a couple of hours before frying.

Deep-fry the croquetas in batches until golden, drain briefly on paper towel and serve immediately.

MAKES 30–35

Spring Rolls chinese pickled + mushroom
praw spring voll

Raw :- 350g pramns clean chopped.

Panfini clji 2 oil carrots sliced shredded finely
sesame oil/z oil 10 cm Knob ginger julienne.

{ 8 sliced small mushroom.
  8 shitaked . sliced .
  2 clove garlic finely choppd.
  1 table spoon oil : grape.
  1/2 tea spoon sesame.
  1 table chines rice wine : wimen.

— cabbage pickeld
— fennel
— dikon

Iceberg.

Prawn & Mushroom Spring Rolls with Chinese Pickles

*I'm a sucker for a spring roll, and especially a prawn spring roll. This version evolved out of having a little rainbow of homemade **Spiced Chinese Pickles** (page 46) at my disposal. The sweet vinegary punch works so well with the crunchy wrappers, succulent prawns and hints of warm spice. These are delicious with **Spiced Blood Plum Sauce** (page 34) and a few extra pickles on the side, or try them with a sprinkling of **Sichuan & Mandarin Salt** (page 24). Be warned, though, these are a bit of a labour of love and will be devoured in a flash.*

PRAWN & MUSHROOM SPRING ROLLS WITH CHINESE PICKLES

1 tablespoon grapeseed oil (or other neutral oil)

1 teaspoon sesame oil

10-cm piece of ginger, julienned

2 carrots, julienned

8 small Swiss brown mushrooms, diced

8 shiitake mushrooms, finely sliced

2 tablespoons rice wine vinegar

1 handful each of daikon, wombok and fennel Spiced Chinese Pickles (page 46), well drained

350 g green prawn cutlets, deveined and chopped

3 tablespoons light soy sauce

1½ tablespoons cornflour

¼ teaspoon Chinese five-spice

¼ teaspoon white pepper

oil, for deep-frying

20 spring roll wrappers

1 eggwhite, lightly whisked

Spiced Blood Plum Sauce (page 34), to serve

Place a wok or large frying pan over high heat. Add half the grapeseed oil, half the sesame oil and the ginger and stir-fry for 1 minute. Add the carrot and stir-fry for 2 minutes. Tip out of the wok into a large bowl and set aside.

Add the remaining grapeseed and sesame oil to the wok, follow with the mushrooms and stir-fry for 3 minutes. Add the vinegar, cook for 1 minute and then tip into the bowl with the carrot.

Press out all the liquid from the pickles and drain on paper towel. Slice into a rough julienne and add to the bowl along with the prawn meat.

Combine the soy, cornflour, five-spice and white pepper in a small bowl and add to the mix. Combine well using your hands.

Preheat a deep-fryer or saucepan of oil to 175°C.

Place a spring roll wrapper on the bench and brush three sides with eggwhite. Spoon 1½ tablespoons of filling along the length adjacent to the un-brushed edge, leaving enough space at each end to enclose the mix. Fold the un-brushed edge over and pull back tightly to form a firm log. Continue to roll up, folding the ends in once half rolled. Seal with more eggwhite and press down firmly to form a flat seam. Repeat for the remaining mix.

Fry five to six spring rolls at a time for about 4 minutes until golden and very crisp. Drain on paper towel and serve immediately with the plum sauce or a spicy sweet chilli sauce on the side.

MAKES 20

*Empanadas make brilliant party food, are perfect for school or work lunchboxes, and make a great snack at the football or soccer (and they're just as good if you're watching the game on TV). You can fill these with anything you like, but they're particularly delicious with sausage ragu, chopped egg and briny green olives. You could also fill these with my **Bolognaise-style Mushroom Ragu** (page 180) and a little Manchego or ricotta cheese. The empanadas can be frozen before they're cooked, simply thaw on the bench for 30 minutes before baking.*

EMPANADAS WITH SAUSAGE RAGU, EGG & OLIVES

400 g Sausage Ragu (page 213)

4 hard-boiled eggs, chopped

1 handful of pitted olives, chopped

1 teaspoon sweet paprika, plus extra

1 egg, beaten

freshly ground black pepper

DOUGH

2 extra-large eggs

125 ml ice-cold water

1 teaspoon white vinegar

480 g plain flour, plus extra

1 teaspoon salt

80 g very cold butter, finely diced

For the dough, add the eggs, iced water and vinegar to a small bowl and whisk until combined. Combine the flour and salt in a large bowl. Add the butter and rub into the flour with your fingers until incorporated. Make a well in the mix, pour in the liquid and mix with a fork to form a dough. The dough shouldn't be sticky, so add a little more flour if necessary. Turn out onto a floured bench and knead for a couple of minutes until smooth. Wrap the dough in plastic wrap and refrigerate for 30 minutes.

Preheat the oven to 180°C fan-forced (200°C conventional). Line two baking trays with baking paper.

For the filling, combine the ragu, chopped egg, olives and 1 teaspoon of paprika in a medium bowl.

Cut the rested dough into eighteen even pieces and roll into balls. Roll each ball into a 3–4-mm thick disc using a rolling pin. Place 1 heaped tablespoon of filling on each disc, fold the edges together and crimp to seal. Transfer the empanadas to the prepared trays and brush the top of each with beaten egg. Sprinkle over a little extra paprika, grind over some pepper and bake for about 12 minutes until golden.

MAKES 18

Empanadas with Sausage Ragu, Egg & Olives

Innocuous looking steamed bao invaded kitchens a little while back, kicking even tacos off the fashionable table, and it looks like they're here to stay. I really do love super-light freshly steamed bao, especially filled with sticky, slow-roasted pork, earthy chilli sauce, toasty sesame mayo and a refreshing foil of cucumber, coriander and peppery cress. A sliver of **Watermelon Rind Pickle** *(page 39) would also work well.*

Cooking off a whole slab of pork belly and a big batch of bao may seem like a lot of food – well, it is – but it's amazing how quickly these vanish. If your crowd is not quite up to the challenge, leftover buns will freeze well and the pork is great with rice and steamed greens, or in fried rice, **Congee** *(page 172) or a* **Bánh Mì** *(pages 146–7).*

SPICED PORK BELLY BAO WITH SESAME MAYONNAISE & GOCHUJANG

1 × 1.5–1.8 kg boneless pork belly from the thick end, skin scored

2 tablespoons vegetable oil

2 tablespoons salt flakes

1 large continental cucumber

1 quantity steamed Bao (page 85)

½ quantity Gochujang Chilli Sauce (page 40)

1 bunch of watercress, picked

½ bunch of coriander, leaves picked

SPICED HONEY GLAZE

115 g fragrant honey

2 garlic cloves, skin on, lightly bruised

2 fresh bay leaves

2 star anise

2 tablespoons coriander seeds, cracked

1 tablespoon Sichuan peppercorns

SESAME MAYONNAISE

125 g Mayonnaise (for a recipe, see page 31)

2 tablespoons sesame seeds, toasted and ground

1 tablespoon rice wine vinegar

1 teaspoon sesame oil

Preheat the oven to 160°C fan-forced (180°C conventional).

Rub the pork well with the oil and salt and place, skin-side up, on a rack above a roasting tray. Pour 800 ml of water into the tray and roast for 2½ hours. If necessary, increase the temperature to 200°C fan-forced (220°C conventional) for the last 20 minutes to crisp up the skin.

Meanwhile, for the sesame mayonnaise, combine all the ingredients in a small bowl and refrigerate until needed.

Trim the cucumber and cut into three even lengths. Finely slice each piece lengthways on a mandoline.

For the glaze, add all the ingredients to a small saucepan and simmer for 2 minutes.

Once the pork is cooked, pour the roasting juices from the tray into a jug and skim off the fat. Add about half the juices to the glaze and simmer for 4 minutes until slightly thickened. Pour the glaze over the pork and set aside to rest for 10–15 minutes.

Slice the pork into 2-cm thick slices and cut each slice into four.

To assemble, smother the base of the freshly steamed bao with the gochujang sauce and follow with a piece of pork. Top with a slice of cucumber, a little watercress, some coriander and a dollop of sesame mayonnaise. Serve immediately.

MAKES ABOUT 35

Spiced Pork Belly

*The lobster roll or New England lobster roll – named after their birthplace on the American east coast where lobsters are pretty plentiful (and just a little bit cheaper than here) – has captured the public imagination like few other sandwiches. My version takes a detour into Korean cuisine with the addition of a little **Kimchi** (page 47), though you could definitely leave it out. I also like the nutty and toasty richness of sesame seeds in the mayonnaise for this, as well as plenty of chopped egg – a bit of a reference to* salade à la russe, *one of my favourite ways with cray.*

BRIOCHE ROLLS WITH CRAYFISH, KIMCHI & SESAME MAYONNAISE

4 Brioche rolls (pages 92–3), cut open lengthways

¼ iceberg lettuce, shredded

400 g cooked crayfish meat, sliced into 5-mm thick medallions

salt flakes

100 g Kimchi (page 47), finely chopped

½ lemon

1 tablespoon black sesame seeds

1 tablespoon white sesame seeds

SESAME MAYONNAISE

2 extra-large eggs, at room temperature

125 g Mayonnaise (for a recipe, see page 31)

2 tablespoons sesame seeds, toasted and ground

1 tablespoon rice wine vinegar

1 teaspoon sesame oil

For the sesame mayonnaise, carefully lower the eggs into a saucepan of simmering water and cook for 6 minutes. Lift from the water, refresh under cold water and peel. Chop the eggs and combine with the remaining ingredients in a small bowl.

Smother the brioche with the sesame mayonnaise and top with the lettuce and crayfish. Season with salt flakes, then add the kimchi. Squeeze over a little lemon juice, sprinkle over the sesame seeds and serve.

SERVES 4

One of the world's best sandwiches – a beautifully simple affair of grilled fish with lettuce, softened onions and lemon in a crusty, soft-centred roll – is sold under and around Istanbul's famous Galata Bridge. The best vendors, well the ones I was drawn to, were grilling the fish – what looked like blue mackerel – over coals, elevating it even further with a little char and the subtle scent of smoke. The heat and juices from the fish soften the bread and the whole lot just kind of melds together into one of those unforgettable food moments. Inspired by that sandwich, this version takes a slightly different route using fried calamari, a spike of chilli, the lemony tang of sumac and soft pide, but the spirit is there, and besides, there's always room for another great sandwich.

GALATA BRIDGE SANDWICH

1 small white onion, very finely sliced into rings

2 teaspoons sumac, plus extra

oil, for deep-frying

100 g plain flour

150 g fine semolina

salt flakes and freshly ground black pepper

3 small soft pides, spilt open

¼ iceberg lettuce, finely shredded

450 g cleaned calamari, wings attached, sliced into thin rings, tentacles divided into pairs

1 lemon

1 long green chilli, finely sliced

PAPRIKA AIOLI

200 g Mayonnaise (for a recipe, see page 31)

1 large garlic clove, finely grated or crushed

2 pinches of mild smoked paprika

Soak the onion in cold water for 10 minutes. Drain, pat dry with paper towel and toss with 2 teaspoons of sumac.

For the paprika aioli, combine all the ingredients in a small bowl.

Preheat a deep-fryer or 3 cm of oil in a large, deep-sided frying pan to 180°C.

Combine the flour, semolina and 1 teaspoon of salt flakes in a large bowl.

Toast the bread and generously smear the bottom halves with the aioli. Top with the onion and lettuce.

Toss the calamari in the flour mix until well coated, gently shake off any excess and fry in batches for 2–3 minutes until lightly golden. Drain briefly on paper towel and season lightly.

Pile the calamari on top of the lettuce, squeeze over a little lemon, sprinkle over some chilli and extra sumac and close the sandwiches. Cut each sandwich in half and serve immediately.

SERVES 6

Korean fried chicken or, as it's commonly known, the other KFC, has become something of a cult food of late, right up there with pulled pork and fish tacos. Anyone for succulent fried chicken covered in golden batter that's surrendering to a drenching slick of sticky, hot and sweet chilli sauce? It's really not that hard to love.

Don't worry about the batter clumping rather than coating the chicken evenly, as it gives the chicken plenty of crunchy irregular edges to take up the sauce. It's important to add the cooked chicken to the sauce all in one go; if you add the chicken bit by bit, the first batch can soak up more sauce than it needs, leaving the last a little short. Please serve as soon as the chicken is dressed, as the batter will soften and you'll miss the magic – and don't forget the cold beers and plenty of napkins!

KOREAN-STYLE FRIED CHICKEN

oil, for deep-frying

3 eggwhites

3 teaspoons salt flakes

100 g sweet rice flour, plus extra

50 g potato starch

50 g plain flour

1 teaspoon bicarbonate of soda

2 teaspoons freshly ground black pepper

16 chicken wings, drumettes and wings separated, wing tips left on

3 tablespoons toasted sesame seeds

4 spring onions, finely sliced

CHILLI SAUCE

½ cup gochujang (see note on page 40)

3 garlic cloves, finely grated

10-cm piece of ginger, finely grated

80 g dark brown sugar

80 ml dark soy sauce

80 ml rice vinegar

2½ tablespoons fish sauce

1 tablespoon sesame oil

Preheat a deep-fryer or 15 cm of oil in a large saucepan to 170°C.

For the chilli sauce, add all the ingredients to a medium saucepan and simmer for 4 minutes until slightly thickened. Tip into a large bowl.

Whisk the eggwhites in a large bowl until foaming. Whisk in 200 ml of water and the salt. Sift in 100 g of rice flour, the potato starch, plain flour, bicarbonate of soda and pepper and mix until a smooth batter forms.

Dust the chicken in a little extra rice flour, shaking off any excess, and add to the batter. Mix through until well coated.

Fry the chicken in batches for 7 minutes each. Drain on paper towel and set aside, keeping the batches separate.

Once all the chicken has been cooked, starting with the first batch, fry for another 7 minutes, or until golden and cooked through. Drain again, keeping the first batch warm while you fry the second.

Once all the chicken has been cooked a second time, add all of it to the sauce and toss until thoroughly coated. Serve immediately with a sprinkling of sesame seeds and spring onion.

SERVES 4

CHICKEN

As with laying hens (see page 71), birds reared for their meat are better for us if they've had a good chance to grow at a natural rate while scratching around in pasture eating grubs, bugs, worms and seeds – they also have better flavour and texture. Due to intensive farming methods, chicken has become so inexpensive that a lovingly reared chook can seem outrageously expensive when compared to the supermarket staple, but twenty or so dollars for a chicken that can feed a family and then the bones used to make a nutritious stock (page 52) hardly seems unreasonable. I always buy a whole bird, and if I'm not going to roast it just like that, I'll break it down and freeze the trimmings – wingtips, backbone, frame and any other bits and pieces – to use in stocks and sauces.

*The bánh mì tells quite a story in one little sandwich: colonialism, revolution and plenty of adaptability. Besides the history lesson, they're pretty darn tasty. This mightn't be a task you'd set for yourself from scratch, but it is a pretty delicious way to use up some leftover **Spiced Pork Belly** (page 137) or roast chook. However, if you have to cater for more than the average number of guests, setting up a little production line of these and cutting them in half to serve would be a pretty effective way of making lots of people happy in a fairly short amount of time. They're great for a picnic, too. The filling ingredients below are suggestions and you can adapt them to your needs, just make sure there's plenty of freshness and a bit of heat. And don't, under any circumstances, try using more 'fashionable' bread for these!*

BÁNH MÌ

CORIANDER & BLACK PEPPER TOFU

⅓ cup Sesame Mayonnaise (page 137)

4 long white Vietnamese rolls, cut open lengthways

¼ iceberg lettuce, finely shredded

1 Lebanese cucumber, finely sliced lengthways

2 tomatoes, sliced

2 carrots, julienned and softened with a little salt or fish sauce

2–3 pieces of daikon from Spiced Chinese Pickles (page 46), julienned

salt flakes and ground white pepper

2 handfuls of coriander leaves

2 bird's eye chillies, sliced

2 handfuls of mustard cress or watercress

⅓ cup Spiced Blood Plum Sauce (page 34)

CORIANDER & BLACK PEPPER TOFU

80 ml grapeseed oil (or other neutral oil)

4 garlic cloves, sliced

2 teaspoons coriander seeds, roughly ground

1 teaspoon ground black pepper

1 × 300–350 g packet firm tofu, cut into domino-sized pieces

1 tablespoon fish sauce

1 tablespoon light soy sauce

For the tofu, add the oil to a large frying pan or wok over medium heat. Add the garlic and fry until golden. Add the coriander seeds, pepper and tofu and stir-fry for 3 minutes. Add the fish and soy sauces and take off the heat.

Smear the sesame mayonnaise down the length of each roll and follow with the lettuce, cucumber, tomato, carrot and daikon, season with salt and pepper and top with the coriander, chilli, cress, hot tofu and plum sauce.

SERVES 4

PORK BELLY

2 tablespoons Chicken Liver
Parfait (pages 202–3)

4 long white Vietnamese rolls, cut
open lengthways

¼ iceberg lettuce, finely
shredded

1 Lebanese cucumber, finely
sliced lengthways

2 tomatoes, sliced

2 carrots, julienned and softened
with a little salt or fish sauce

2–3 pieces of daikon from
Spiced Chinese Pickles
(page 46), julienned

salt flakes and ground white
pepper

2 handfuls of coriander leaves

2 bird's eye chillies, sliced

2 handfuls of mustard cress or
watercress

4 slices of Spiced Pork Belly
(page 137)

⅓ cup Spiced Blood Plum Sauce
(page 34)

Smear the parfait down the length of each roll and follow with
the lettuce, cucumber, tomato, carrot and daikon, season with salt
and pepper and top with the coriander, chilli, cress, pork belly and
plum sauce.

SERVES 4

CHICKEN

2 tablespoons Chicken Liver
Parfait (pages 202–3)

4 long white Vietnamese rolls, cut
open lengthways

¼ iceberg lettuce, finely
shredded

1 Lebanese cucumber, finely
sliced lengthways

2 tomatoes, sliced

2 carrots, julienned and softened
with a little salt or fish sauce

2–3 pieces of daikon from
Spiced Chinese Pickles
(page 46), julienned

salt flakes and ground white
pepper

2 handfuls of coriander leaves

2 bird's eye chillies, sliced

2 handfuls of mustard cress or
watercress

1 handful of shiso leaves

2 handfuls of shredded cooked
chicken

⅓ cup Spiced Blood Plum Sauce
(page 34)

⅓ cup Sesame Mayonnaise
(page 137)

1 handful of salted peanuts,
smashed

Smear the parfait down the length of each roll and follow with the
lettuce, cucumber, tomato, carrot and daikon, season with salt and
pepper and top with the coriander, chilli, cress, shiso, chicken, plum
sauce, sesame mayonnaise and smashed peanuts.

SERVES 4

Pork Belly Bánh Mì

Chicken Bánh Mì

*Coriander & Black
Pepper Tofu Bánh Mì*

These sticky lamb ribs are great for entertaining, a perfect platter to hand around a hungry crowd – just make sure you've got plenty of napkins handy! The miso and ale add deep and darkly mysterious notes to the ribs, while the vinegar helps to cut through the fat. And although you could leave the radishes and pickles off the plate, I think the rich ribs really benefit from a little crunchy fresh relief.

LAMB RIBS WITH MISO, CHILLI & DARK ALE

20 lamb ribs, some of the fat trimmed but not all

2 tablespoons white miso paste

2 teaspoons chilli powder

2 teaspoons salt flakes

3 tablespoons treacle

120 ml apple cider vinegar

200 ml dark ale

2 handfuls of daikon from Spiced Chinese Pickles (page 46)

1 bunch of radishes, cut in half with some stalk left on

Preheat the oven to 180°C fan-forced (200°C conventional).

Add the ribs, miso, chilli powder and salt to a large baking dish and toss to coat. Drizzle over the treacle and pour over the vinegar and ale. Cover with baking paper and foil, seal well and bake for 1 hour. Uncover the ribs, skim the fat off if desired, and cook for a further 20 minutes until dark and crispy. You can colour them up further by turning on the oven grill for a few minutes, but just watch carefully to make sure they don't burn.

Arrange the ribs on a serving platter with the pickled daikon and the radish on the side and serve immediately.

SERVES 8–10

MISO

Miso paste is made from fermented soy beans. It is obviously integral to Japanese cuisine, but it's also an amazingly versatile ingredient that can add umami-laced depth to dishes without necessarily skewing them in an Asian direction. Chefs are increasingly using miso, as well as fish sauce and soy, to subtly layer flavour into sauces, marinades and broths. The key with this is to boost the intensity and complexity of a dish, while keeping the distinctive flavour obscured. Sometimes I can be a bit of a purist with such extreme cross-cultural cooking, but by adding it in small amounts while tasting, you can boost the flavour and depth of say an Italian meat ragu without losing its identity. Miso is particularly good in richer braises and marinades, and is a handy way to fill in a flavour hole when you don't have time for long slow cooking.

When I was growing up, I would have traded in my after-school snack of soft peanut butter sandwich and glass of milk for this in a flash, though I won't be making these a regular part of my girls' diets! Yes, these are a little indulgent, but there's no point doing these things by halves, just reserve them as special treats – that goes for adults, too.

PEANUT BUTTER COOKIE ICE CREAM SANDWICHES

1 litre vanilla ice cream

300 g dark chocolate, chopped

200 g salted peanuts, roughly chopped

Himalayan salt or sea salt flakes (optional)

COOKIES

230 g plain flour

190 g rolled oats

1 teaspoon baking powder

1 teaspoon bicarbonate of soda

225 ml milk

125 g natural yoghurt

260 g smooth peanut butter

60 g unsalted butter

150 g brown sugar

½ teaspoon salt flakes

2 extra-large eggs

chopped salted peanuts, to decorate

Preheat the oven to 175°C fan-forced (195°C conventional). Line two baking trays with baking paper.

To make the cookies, add the flour, oats, baking powder and bicarbonate of soda to a food processor and blitz to a fine crumb.

Combine the milk and yoghurt in a bowl or jug.

Add the peanut butter, butter, sugar and salt to the bowl of a stand mixer and cream with the paddle attachment for 5 minutes on high speed. Add one egg, followed by the other once the first is fully incorporated. Add half the flour and oat crumbs and combine on low speed. Gradually add the milk and yoghurt mixture until incorporated. Add the remaining flour and oat crumbs and mix until combined. Transfer the batter to a piping bag fitted with a large, plain nozzle.

Pipe dollops of batter about the size of a fifty-cent piece and about 2-cm thick on the prepared trays, leaving enough space between each and the lip of the tray to allow for spreading (you will probably need to do this in a couple of batches). Top with some chopped peanuts and bake for 13 minutes until lightly golden. Set aside to cool completely on wire racks. They will be soft and spongy.

To make the ice cream sandwiches, add a small scoop of ice cream to the flat side of a biscuit, top with the flat side of another biscuit and firmly but carefully press the two together until the ice cream is evenly spread to the edges. Place in the freezer for 20 minutes to chill. Repeat for the remaining biscuits.

Gently melt the chocolate in a bowl sitting in another bowl of tap-hot water.

Roll the edges of the chilled sandwiches through the chopped peanuts to coat the exposed ice cream, and then dip one side of the biscuit into the chocolate. Sprinkle a little salt (if using) onto the chocolate and serve.

MAKES ABOUT 20

This is a really easy recipe that produces especially light and fluffy doughnuts, but not at the expense of substance. I like these freshly fried and rolled in the spiced sugar, but going the extra step by making the dulce de leche makes them extra special and pretty indulgent – a good thing, I think. You could also glaze these with a simple icing sugar mix flavoured with vanilla extract or fresh berry or citrus juice.

DOUGHNUTS WITH CINNAMON & CLOVE SUGAR & DULCE DE LECHE

230 ml milk
14 g (2 sachets) dried yeast
40 g light muscovado sugar
200 g unsalted butter, softened
4 extra-large eggs, whisked
500 g plain flour
2 pinches of salt flakes
oil, for deep-frying

SPICED SUGAR
300 g caster sugar
3 teaspoons ground cinnamon
2 teaspoons ground cloves

DULCE DE LECHE
1 × 395 g can condensed milk
salt flakes

This recipe is best started the day before serving.

Warm the milk gently in a small saucepan. Turn off the heat, mix in the yeast and half the sugar and set aside until the mix begins to froth.

Add the butter and the remaining sugar to the bowl of a stand mixer and cream using the whisk attachment. Add the eggs in three to four batches while beating, waiting until each is incorporated before adding the next. Add the yeast mix and beat until combined. Switch the whisk for a paddle, add the flour and salt and mix until smooth. Transfer to a container and prove overnight in the fridge, or for at least 4 hours.

For the dulce de leche, place the unopened can of condensed milk in a large saucepan with plenty of water and bring to a simmer. Reduce the heat to very low, cover the pan with a lid and cook for 3 hours. Turn off the heat and stand for 2 hours to cool before removing the lid. Carefully open the cooled can and pour the caramel into a bowl. Whisk in a little salt and 150 ml of boiling water until smooth. This will keep for a couple of months in the refrigerator, simply warm through to loosen.

Preheat a deep-fryer or saucepan of oil to 170°C.

For the spiced sugar, combine all the ingredients in a large bowl.

Tip the risen dough out onto a lightly floured bench and roll out until 1.5-cm thick. Cut out rounds – you can make these any size you like and leave them whole or cut out the middle – and immediately lift onto a piece of floured baking paper, being careful as the dough will be quite wet. Cook the first batch as soon as they're cut, frying for 2 minutes on each side (hole-less doughnuts will take a little longer, and the cut-outs will take about half the time), and drain well on paper towel. You can re-roll any leftover

scraps once more, but they will lose too much aeration if you roll them again. Once drained, toss the hot doughnuts in the sugar mix until well coated and serve warm with the dulce de leche.

MAKES ABOUT 20

PASTA, DUMPLINGS, NOODLES & RICE

FLAVOURS FROM AROUND THE WORLD

BEEF PHO

**STIR-FRIED PORK & PRAWN WONTONS
WITH KALE & WATER CHESTNUTS**

SHOYU RAMEN

SINGAPORE NOODLES WITH PRAWNS & ROAST DUCK

BIBIMBAP

CONGEE

**RICOTTA RAVIOLI WITH ROASTED TOMATO SAUCE
& SHAVED FENNEL**

**KALE & SPINACH GNUDI WITH BURNT BUTTER,
SAGE, LEMON & WALNUTS**

BOLOGNAISE-STYLE MUSHROOM RAGU

**EGG, TOMATO & SPINACH CURRY WITH
GINGER & TURMERIC**

**SOUR FISH & OKRA CURRY WITH BAKED
COCONUT & LEMON RICE**

ROGAN JOSH

Before our girls arrived on the scene, Mike and I would go out for beef pho (beef noodle soup) almost every week. We'd start with a round of crunchy spring rolls wrapped in crisp lettuce and Vietnamese mint, a cold beer, a little tea and then straight into the fragrant soup. Mike would usually have to ask for more bean sprouts, as I'd tend to get through a bit more than my share, maybe another beer, and that's it. And not much has changed now. The girls have enjoyed the broth since they were toddlers, and are now starting to play around with some herbs and a little chilli. And they've insisted on their own bowls for some time now. I genuinely crave pho no matter how I'm feeling, but if I'm a little under the weather, a hot bowl laden with fresh herbs and plenty of chilli is the most soothing thing I can imagine. This version is inspired by the beautiful pho at Thanh Phong on Victoria Street in Richmond, my favourite for the last fifteen or so years.

BEEF PHO

225 g sirloin steak
1 kg fresh rice noodles
1 bunch of Thai basil
250 g bean sprouts
lemon wedges, to serve
sliced bird's eye chillies, to serve
1 white onion, finely sliced

BROTH
2 onions, skin on, cut in half
15-cm piece of ginger, cut into 5 thick slices
1.5 kg beef bone, preferably from the joint
1.5 kg beef shin, bone in
1 x 800 g trimmed brisket
8 spring onions, cut into batons
1 garlic bulb, cut in half horizontally
1 tablespoon salt flakes
5 star anise
2 tablespoons coriander seeds
1½ tablespoons fennel seeds
1½ tablespoons black peppercorns
10-cm piece of cassia bark
80 g palm sugar (choose a light coloured one, or it will darken the broth), plus extra
3 tablespoons fish sauce, plus extra

To prepare the broth, blacken the onion and ginger over a naked flame, or on a baking tray under a hot grill for about 15 minutes.

Place the beef bone and shin in a large saucepan and cover with cold water. Bring to the boil and cook vigorously for 3 minutes. Drain and rinse under warm water.

Wipe out the pan and return the bone and shin. Add the brisket and 6 litres of water and bring to the boil. Reduce to a gentle simmer and cook for about 10 minutes, skimming off any scum from the surface as it appears. Add the blackened onion and ginger, the spring onion, garlic, salt and spices and simmer very gently for 1½ hours, skimming occasionally.

Remove the brisket after 1½ hours, it should be tender but still a little chewy, and place in cold water for 5 minutes. Drain, wrap the meat in plastic wrap and refrigerate.

Continue to cook the broth at a very gentle simmer, skimming occasionally, for a further 2 hours. Strain, discard the solids and refrigerate the broth. Once cooled, the fat will form a layer on top of the liquid, discard this.

To serve, reheat the broth and stir through 80 g of palm sugar and 3 tablespoons of fish sauce. Adjust with more sugar and fish sauce to taste. Keep the broth at a simmer.

Unwrap the brisket and slice finely. Slice the sirloin finely across the grain.

Gently loosen the noodles in your hands and add to a large bowl. Cover with boiling water, stand for 2 minutes and then drain.

Arrange the basil, bean sprouts, lemon and chilli in separate piles on a serving platter.

Divide the noodles between serving bowls and arrange the brisket, sirloin and onion on top. Ladle over the hot broth and serve with the platter on the side for your guests to add to the broth as they like.

SERVES 6

Kale might not be the first vegetable you'd think of using for a dish like this, but it works wonderfully well. The chewy, textural quality of the kale is a great contrast to the slippery, silky wontons, and the deep vegetal flavour really stands up to the rich cooking sauce.

*This wonton recipe is easily doubled (just add a whole egg rather than another eggwhite) if you wanted to make a big batch for larger scale entertaining. Just sprinkle over some spring onion and **Sichuan & Mandarin Salt** (page 24), and make a dipping sauce with soy, vinegar and a little chilli. You can also deep-fry them, if you prefer.*

½ bunch of kale, leaves stripped

2 tablespoons grapeseed oil (or other neutral oil)

100 g ginger, julienned

4 garlic cloves, finely sliced

120 g water chestnuts, sliced

2 handfuls of Thai basil leaves

1 teaspoon Sichuan & Mandarin Salt (page 24)

COOKING SAUCE

150 ml oyster sauce

80 ml light soy sauce

80 ml Shaoxing cooking wine

1 teaspoon sesame oil

1 teaspoon caster sugar

½ teaspoon white pepper

PORK & PRAWN WONTONS

1 corn cob

150 g finely ground pork mince

150 g green prawn cutlets, deveined and roughly chopped

3 spring onions, finely sliced

25 g ginger, finely grated

1 large garlic clove, finely grated

1¼ tablespoons soy sauce

1¼ tablespoons Shaoxing cooking wine

¾ teaspoon sesame oil

½ teaspoon ground white pepper

2 eggwhites, kept separate

1½ tablespoons cornflour, plus extra for dusting

25–30 large square wonton wrappers

STIR-FRIED PORK & PRAWN WONTONS WITH KALE & WATER CHESTNUTS

For the wontons, cook the corn in boiling salted water for 5 minutes. Once cool enough to handle, slice the kernels off and chop well.

Add the chopped corn to a medium bowl with the pork, prawn meat, spring onion, ginger, garlic, soy, Shaoxing wine, sesame oil, white pepper, 1 eggwhite and 1½ tablespoons of cornflour and combine well with your hands.

Lay a wonton skin on the bench and brush two adjacent edges with a little beaten eggwhite. Add 2 teaspoons of the filling and fold into a triangular parcel, pressing the edges together to seal. Place on a plate dusted with cornflour and repeat until the filling is used up.

Blanch the kale in boiling salted water for 3 minutes. Drain well and squeeze out any excess moisture.

Combine all the cooking sauce ingredients in a small bowl.

Cook the wontons in two batches in simmering salted water for 5 minutes each. Lift out carefully and place in a warm, lightly oiled dish.

Heat a large frying pan or wok until very hot. Add the oil, ginger and garlic and stir-fry for 1 minute. Add the water chestnuts and kale and stir-fry for 3 minutes. Add the wontons and cooking sauce and cook for about 2 minutes, tossing to coat. Lift the wontons out of the pan onto a serving plate. Reduce the liquid briefly until slightly thickened and pour over the platter. Scatter over the basil leaves, sprinkle over the Sichuan salt and serve.

SERVES 4

NANAMI TOGARASHI

Nanami togarashi (or shichimi togarashi) is a Japanese spice mix of coarse chilli flakes typically supported by sansho pepper, dried orange or mandarin peel, black and white sesame seeds, nori and ground ginger. It's great to have on hand to add a little spice and umami lift to noodle dishes, broths and salads.

A really good bowl of ramen can be a truly magical thing – no wonder it inspires such obsessive fans. This version requires a bit of effort, but the results are absolutely stunning. I'm usually a big fan of the noodles in a bowl of ramen, but this stock is so deeply and mysteriously flavoured that I could drink it practically every day just on its own.

SHOYU RAMEN

800 g boned pork shoulder or scotch fillet, rolled and tied

2 tablespoons grapeseed oil (or other neutral oil)

salt flakes and ground white pepper

1 teaspoon bicarbonate of soda

800 g dried wavy ramen noodles

4 extra-large eggs, at room temperature

4 spring onions, white and pale green parts, finely sliced on an angle

2 pickled bamboo shoots, finely sliced

150 g bean sprouts

4 shiitake mushrooms, sliced

black sesame seeds, to serve

nanami togarashi (see left), to serve

chilli oil, to serve

2 sheets of roasted nori, torn

STOCK

50 g dried kombu

150 g double-smoked bacon rashers

150 g carrots (about 2), split lengthways

150 g French shallots (about 4), skin on, cut in half

3 large garlic cloves, skin on, smashed

80 g ginger, cut into chunks

30 g bonito flakes

10 g dried shiitake mushrooms (about 6)

TARE

80 ml quality aged soy sauce

2 tablespoons mirin

2 tablespoons sake

For the stock, add the kombu and 4.5 litres of boiling water to a large saucepan and set aside for 1 hour.

Rub the pork with the oil and season with salt and white pepper. Heat a large, non-stick frying pan over medium heat. Brown the pork, skin-side down first, for about 10–12 minutes, turning regularly for an even crust.

Add the pork and the remaining stock ingredients to the pan with the kombu stock. Bring to the boil and immediately reduce the heat. Simmer for 10 minutes, skimming the surface of impurities as they appear. Cover with a lid and simmer gently for about 1 hour until the pork is tender.

Remove the cooked pork from the liquid and set aside to cool slightly. Strain the stock through a fine sieve and discard the solids. Once the pork is cool to the touch, wrap tightly in three layers of plastic wrap and refrigerate until firm, about 1½–2 hours.

For the tare, combine all the ingredients in a small bowl.

Add the strained stock and tare to a large saucepan and simmer very slowly for 20 minutes.

Meanwhile, bring a medium saucepan of water to a rolling boil, add the bicarbonate of soda and noodles and cook for 3–4 minutes. Drain and set aside.

Gently lower the eggs into simmering water and cook for 5 minutes for soft boiled, or 7 minutes for hard boiled. Refresh in cold water, peel and cut in half.

Unwrap the chilled pork and slice finely.

Divide the noodles between serving bowls and arrange the pork slices on top. Cover with the very hot stock and top with the spring onion, bamboo shoots, bean sprouts, mushrooms, eggs and sesame seeds. Serve immediately with the nanami togarashi, chilli oil and torn nori on the side.

SERVES 6

Shoyu Ramen Stock

*Even though the name suggests otherwise, this isn't exactly a classic Singaporean dish. It was apparently developed by Cantonese chefs who were inspired by the diversity of the tiny republic – I guess that's how the curry powder fits in. Either way, it's pretty delicious and can be as simple or as complicated as you want to make it. This version calls for Chinese roast duck, which could be a good way to use up some leftovers, or you could use roast chicken or pork instead – leftover **Spiced Pork Belly** (page 137) or pork shoulder from the **Bo Ssam** (pages 232–3) would be perfect.*

SINGAPORE NOODLES WITH PRAWNS & ROAST DUCK

200 g rice vermicelli

1 tablespoon Malaysian curry powder

100 ml light soy sauce

100 ml rice wine

2 teaspoons caster sugar

2 large garlic cloves, sliced

2 tablespoons finely grated ginger

1 long green chilli, finely chopped

3 spring onions, white and pale green parts, cut into 4-cm batons

1 handful of green beans, finely sliced into rounds

½ red capsicum, finely sliced

4 shiitake mushrooms, sliced

6 water chestnuts, sliced

50 g peas

¼ wombok, shredded

½ Chinese roast duck, meat and skin picked and shredded

6 large green prawn cutlets, deveined and finely chopped

2 tablespoons peanut oil (or other neutral oil)

2 eggs, beaten with a pinch of salt

1 handful of coriander leaves

Soak the vermicelli in boiling water for 45 seconds. Drain and set aside in a sieve for about 30 minutes, tossing occasionally to stop the noodles clumping together.

Combine half the curry powder with the soy, rice wine and sugar in a small bowl.

Add the noodles to a large bowl and pour over the curry and soy mix. Toss gently until the noodles are well coated.

So that you can add the ingredients to the hot wok quickly, add the garlic, ginger, chilli, spring onion and the remaining curry powder to one bowl, the beans, capsicum, mushrooms, water chestnuts, peas and wombok to another, and the duck and prawns to a third. Have a small glass or jug of water on hand to add a splash to the wok if the noodles start to dry out.

Heat 1 tablespoon of oil in a wok over high heat until it starts to smoke. Add the garlic and ginger mix and stir-fry for about 30 seconds until fragrant. Add the vegetables, stir-fry for about 2 minutes and tip out into a bowl.

Add the remaining oil to the wok over high heat and add the duck and prawns. Stir-fry for 2–3 minutes, push to the side of the wok and tip in the egg. As the egg sets and starts to stick to the wok, gently scramble it through the duck and prawns. Add the vegetables back to the wok and stir through briefly. Add the noodles and toss for 2–3 minutes to heat the noodles through and ensure that everything is combined, adding a splash of water if necessary. Tip onto a platter, scatter over the coriander and serve.

SERVES 4

Bibimbap is a traditional Korean dish consisting of rice topped with vegetables, egg, gochujang and some form of protein, often beef. The ingredients are kept in more or less separate piles, and the whole lot is stirred together at the table – the name, bibimbap, being made up of the Korean words for mixing and for rice. Some versions call for marinated raw beef and raw egg yolk, which would be especially delicious with some beautiful hand-cut eye fillet, and are often served in super-hot stone or earthenware bowls. This recipe can be altered to your liking, use hard-boiled eggs or raw yolks, try different vegetables, and even swap out the meat for some tofu or tempeh.

BIBIMBAP

650 g scotch fillet, sliced on an angle as finely as possible

200 g baby spinach leaves

150 g bean sprouts

120 ml grapeseed oil (or other neutral oil)

2 large garlic cloves, finely grated

10-cm piece of ginger, julienned

2 teaspoons sesame oil

1 punnet of shiitake mushrooms, sliced

200 g daikon, julienned

1 large carrot, julienned

cooked sushi rice, to serve

6 eggs

5 radishes, finely sliced

2 witlof, trimmed and leaves separated

3 spring onions, white and most of the green, finely sliced

1 tablespoon sesame seeds

1 quantity Gochujang Chilli Sauce (page 40)

MARINADE

3 tablespoons light soy sauce

1 teaspoon sesame oil

1 tablespoon brown sugar

1 tablespoon sesame seeds

1 garlic clove, finely grated

For the marinade, combine all the ingredients in a medium bowl and add the meat. Toss through to coat and set aside for at least 20 minutes.

Bring a large saucepan of salted water to the boil and blanch the spinach for 1 minute. Lift out of the water, drain and squeeze out any water. Blanch the bean sprouts for 30 seconds and drain well.

Heat a large frying pan over high heat. Add a splash of grapeseed oil, a little garlic and ginger and fry briefly until fragrant. Add the bean sprouts and toss through for a few seconds, add a drop of sesame oil, toss and tip out of the pan. Fry the shiitake, daikon, carrot and spinach in separate batches for about 90 seconds each, adding a little oil, garlic and ginger to the pan each time, and finishing with a little sesame oil before tipping out into bowls. Keep all the vegetables separate.

Add some rice to individual serving bowls and arrange the vegetables over the top, keeping them separate and leaving room for the beef.

Fry the eggs in a large non-stick frying pan until the whites are cooked and the yolks are still runny.

While the eggs cook, heat a large frying pan or wok until very hot. Add a splash of grapeseed oil and the beef, spreading it in one layer in the pan. Cook, without stirring, for 2–3 minutes before tossing through quickly and dividing between the bowls.

Finish each portion with an egg, some radish, witlof, spring onion, sesame seeds and a dollop of gochujang sauce. Serve immediately with extra sauce on the side.

SERVES 6

Congee is a particularly comforting and nourishing dish, and one that is traditionally eaten for breakfast or employed to soothe the sick. But it's more versatile than that, and can accommodate endless topping and flavouring additions. With a few choice leftovers, this simple congee can become a quite spectacular lunch or dinner.

*The congee itself is just a starting point, and the additions I've used here are only suggestions. Keep it simple or dress it up as much as you like. This is delicious with **Fried Soft-boiled Eggs** (page 75), leftover pork shoulder from the **Bo Ssam** (pages 232–3) or **Shoyu Ramen** (page 165), **Spiced Pork Belly** (page 137), Chinese duck or pan-fried prawns. Add some prawn crackers or shallow-fried wonton skins for a crunchy textural foil.*

CONGEE

4 extra-large eggs

1 long green chilli, finely sliced

1 long red chilli, finely sliced

80 ml soy sauce

1 teaspoon sesame oil

150 g cooked chicken or pork, sliced or shredded

100 g baby spinach leaves, blanched and drained

8-cm piece of ginger, julienned

4 spring onions, white and pale green parts, finely sliced on an angle

sriracha chilli sauce or Gochujang Chilli Sauce (page 40), to serve

Spiced Chinese Pickles (page 46), to serve

Sichuan & Mandarin Salt (page 24), to serve

CONGEE

250 g sushi rice

2 litres water

1.5 litres chicken stock

1 large piece of dried kombu

2 thick slices of ginger

1 teaspoon salt flakes

For the congee, add all the ingredients to a large, heavy-based saucepan and bring to a simmer. Cook for 45 minutes at a slow simmer, stirring occasionally, until a porridge-like consistency. Remove the kombu once cooked.

Carefully lower the eggs into a saucepan of simmering water and cook for 6 minutes. Refresh in cold water, peel and cut in half.

Combine the chilli, soy and sesame oil in a small bowl.

Divide the congee between serving bowls and top with some chicken or pork, egg, spinach, ginger and spring onion. Serve with the chilli and soy mix, chilli sauce, pickles and Sichuan salt.

SERVES 4

This is such a simple combination of flavours, but one that I just adore – it's my idea of comfort food. I cooked a few versions of pasta with tomato and ricotta during my Melbourne Wine Room days, from a simple bowl of penne pomodoro with some torn basil and a blob of ricotta, to this more refined version. We used to roast trays of late summer tomatoes to concentrate their sun-kissed flavour and add a dimension that you can't get from the pan. We'd keep the sauce very simple, only adding a handful of basil, careful seasoning and a good slick of peppery extra-virgin olive oil. The pasta was always made just before service, and the ravioli filled with milky ricotta even as the first orders were coming in. The cooked pasta was quickly tossed in the sauce and served with fresh fennel, a good grating of Parmigiano-Reggiano and occasionally a sprinkling of dehydrated black olives. Make your own **Fresh Ricotta** *(page 28) for this if you want to go all out.*

PASTA DOUGH

5 extra-large eggs

3 extra-large egg yolks (reserve the eggwhites to seal the ravioli)

2 teaspoons extra-virgin olive oil

500 g plain flour

120 g fine semolina, plus extra

1 pinch of salt flakes

FILLING

450 g Ricotta (for a recipe, see page 28), well drained

50 g Grana Padano, finely grated

2 extra-large eggs, whisked

½ nutmeg, finely grated

salt flakes and freshly ground black pepper

100 g goat's feta, crumbled

ROASTED TOMATO SAUCE

20 ripe roma tomatoes, cored

6 French shallots, sliced into 3-mm thick rounds

6 garlic cloves, sliced

5 thyme sprigs

salt flakes and freshly ground black pepper

170 ml extra-virgin olive oil

10 basil leaves

TO SERVE

1 fennel bulb, finely shaved

100 g Parmigiano-Reggiano, finely grated

RICOTTA RAVIOLI WITH ROASTED TOMATO SAUCE & SHAVED FENNEL

You will need a pasta machine for this recipe.

Preheat the oven to 160°C fan-forced (180°C conventional).

For the sauce, add the tomatoes to a roasting tray that fits them snugly. Scatter over the shallots, garlic and thyme, season generously with salt and pepper and drizzle over 120 ml of oil. Roast for about 1 hour until the tomatoes have collapsed and the shallots and garlic have softened. Set aside to cool.

Pull the skins off the tomatoes and mash the flesh in the tray with your hands. Tip the contents of the tray into a medium saucepan, add the basil and the remaining oil and simmer gently for 15 minutes, stirring regularly. Adjust the seasoning if necessary and set aside.

For the ravioli filling, add the ricotta, Grana Padano, eggs and nutmeg to a medium bowl, season and mix until smooth. Fold the feta through the mix and chill.

For the pasta dough, add the eggs, egg yolks and oil to a medium bowl and whisk until combined. Add the flour, semolina and salt to a food processor and blitz until combined. Pour in the egg mix in a steady and reasonably fast stream while processing. When the mix resembles breadcrumbs, tip out onto the bench and bring together with your hands until an even dough forms. Roll into a log, wrap in plastic wrap and set aside at room temperature for 30 minutes.

Cut the rested dough into six even pieces and press each out flat with your hands. Run each piece of dough through the thickest setting of the pasta machine. Fold each piece in half and run back through the machine, stacking the pieces in a pile as you go. Flip the pile over, turn the pasta machine down one notch and repeat the same process three times, turning the machine down a notch each time. Run the pieces through the machine a few more times, turning down the dial each time but without folding the pasta over itself, until you reach the second finest setting and the pasta is in smooth, long sheets. Sprinkle a little semolina between the sheets and cover with a damp tea towel.

Working in batches, cut the pasta into 10-cm wide strips. Place ¾ tablespoon of filling on each piece and brush around three edges of the filling with eggwhite. Fold the pasta over to enclose the filling and press the edges together to seal, ensuring that there are no air pockets. Trim with a pasta wheel or knife and add to a tray dusted with semolina. Repeat for the remaining pasta and filling.

Reheat the sauce in a large frying pan.

Cook the ravioli in batches in simmering salted water for about 2–3 minutes each. Add to the hot sauce and toss through.

Serve the ravioli with some fennel and a scattering of Parmigiano-Reggiano on top. Serve the remaining cheese on the side.

SERVES 8

OIL

Conventional wisdom says to reserve extra-virgin olive oil for dressings, finishing dishes and the like and to not use it for cooking. The two main reasons here are that it's expensive – fair enough – and that it doesn't tolerate heat well, having a lower smoke point and losing its nutrient value, and even becoming unhealthy in the process. Extra-virgin olive oil actually has a pretty high smoke point, well above what is required for normal cooking, and it's also full of antioxidants that protect the oil and its beneficial properties when heated.

Australian extra-virgin olive oil is a brilliant product that is typically very fresh and far better than the often rancid imported oils found in supermarkets. I personally steer clear of labels that don't bear the mark extra-virgin or virgin, as all other olive oil products have been industrially refined to make them suitable for human consumption. As for vegetable oils and the like, they are quite prone to oxidation and rancidity, and the more often they are reheated the worse this is. I still use neutral oils for certain dishes and for deep-frying, but extra-virgin olive oil does most of the heavy lifting in my kitchen. As for cost, extra-virgin oil is more expensive but it is becoming much more accessibly priced as time goes by, and buying in bulk will dramatically reduce the cost. Naturally, reserve the best fragrant oils to dress and drizzle or just to enjoy with a little good bread.

Ricotta Ravioli with Roasted Tomato Sauce & Shaved Fennel

Gnudi are first cousins of gnocchi, made from fresh ricotta rather than potato. The ricotta makes for an incredibly light and delicate dumpling with a milky richness that doesn't need much embellishment. I love them with just a simple sauce, but this version adds a twist that I find quite delicious. The blanched kale in the gnudi adds a little resistance and chew to the meltingly textural ricotta, making them more robust and just that bit more interesting. Add to this the timeless combination of burnt butter, sage and lemon, plus a handful of walnuts, and you've got yourself a pretty stunning little entree.

KALE & SPINACH GNUDI WITH BURNT BUTTER, SAGE, LEMON & WALNUTS

150 g English spinach leaves

150 g kale leaves

350 g Ricotta (for a recipe, see page 28)

60 g Grana Padano, finely grated

1 egg, lightly beaten

6 grates of nutmeg

salt flakes and freshly ground black pepper

130 g plain flour, plus extra

BURNT BUTTER SAUCE

180 g butter

20 sage leaves

50 g walnuts

salt flakes and freshly ground black pepper

1 lemon

Blanch the spinach in boiling salted water for 3 minutes. Blanch the kale for 5 minutes. Drain both very well, pressing out any excess moisture with your hands. Tip onto a board and chop over finely.

Bring a large saucepan of salted water to a simmer, ready to poach the gnudi.

Add the ricotta, parmesan, egg and nutmeg to a large bowl, season and combine. Gently fold in the kale and spinach mix and follow with the flour. Bring the dough together with your hands and knead for 2 minutes. Using as little extra flour as possible, roll the mix into logs about 3-cm thick. Cut the logs on an angle into 5-cm long pieces.

Poach the gnudi in batches of about ten for 5 minutes each. Lift gently out of the water and add to a baking dish with a little butter. Once all the dumplings have been poached, add them back to the pan in one batch and reheat for 2 minutes. Drain and portion out between warm serving bowls.

For the sauce, melt the butter in a large frying pan until it foams and darkens. As soon as it turns nut-brown, add the sage and walnuts and season with salt and a generous amount of pepper. Toss through for another minute, squeeze in the whole lemon and take off the heat. Stir for 30 seconds, spoon over the gnudi and serve.

SERVES 4

This is a rich and really quite sophisticated mushroom ragu, especially if you're lucky enough to have access to some pine mushrooms, but big meaty field mushrooms will do just fine. The real key to this ragu is in cooking the mushrooms first, which concentrates their flavour and adds roasted notes that you just can't get by sautéing them alone. Also, the dried porcini mushrooms add depth and umami punch to the fresh mushrooms that really cements the intensity of the sauce. Serve this with any pasta – gnocchi and pappardelle are my favourites – or layer into a lasagne.

BOLOGNAISE-STYLE MUSHROOM RAGU

600 g large field mushrooms, cut into rough 3-cm dice

600 g pine mushrooms (or any mushrooms you like, but not Asian ones), cut into rough 3-cm dice

120 ml extra-virgin olive oil

salt flakes and freshly ground black pepper

20 g dried porcini mushrooms

2 onions, diced

8 garlic cloves, finely chopped

3 celery stalks, finely sliced

1 carrot, finely diced

2 fresh bay leaves

½ teaspoon chilli flakes

2 teaspoons fennel seeds

2 tablespoons tomato paste

2 tablespoons red or brown miso paste

400 ml white wine

800 ml chicken or vegetable stock

1 x 400 g can diced tomatoes

1 tablespoon dried Greek oregano

100 g pasta per person

Grana Padano, finely grated, to serve

Preheat the oven to 180°C fan-forced (200°C conventional).

Add the fresh mushrooms to a roasting tray, drizzle over half the oil, season, toss to coat and roast for 20 minutes.

Soak the porcini mushrooms in hot water for 10 minutes. Dice the rehydrated mushrooms and reserve the water.

Heat a large, heavy-based saucepan over medium heat. Add the remaining oil, the onion, garlic, celery, carrot, bay leaves, chilli flakes and fennel seeds and cook for 15 minutes, stirring occasionally. Add the fresh mushrooms and cook, stirring occasionally, for 15 minutes – as the mushrooms sweat down they will help to deglaze the pan. Add the tomato paste and miso and stir constantly for 2 minutes. Add the wine, diced porcini and porcini water and bring to a simmer. Add the stock, tomatoes and oregano and simmer for 45 minutes over low heat until the sauce is thick and intense. Adjust the seasoning to taste.

To serve, cook the pasta according to the packet instructions and toss through the ragu in the pan. Take the pan directly to the table and serve with plenty of Grana Padano on the side.

SERVES 6–8

PINE MUSHROOMS

When I grew up, it was rare to see anything other than a button mushroom make it to the dinner table – even the diminutive champignon versions were somewhat exotic at the time. I do remember, however, people gathering mushrooms by the side of the road and railway line near where we lived. Mum would always say that those orange mushrooms were poisonous, but the foragers obviously knew better and they gathered boxes full of pine mushrooms along with sheaves of wild fennel tops. So many European immigrants simply carried on traditional practices when they came here, and hunting, fishing and foraging would have been an essential part of life for many from rural areas. It took a while before the rest of us caught on, but we did. The days when pine mushrooms were free and calamari was sold as bait are gone! You can, of course, still gather pine mushrooms for free, but just make sure you do it with an experienced guide.

This is a delicious curry that is surprisingly rich, with the yolks adding lusciousness to the sauce when the eggs are broken open. With the baked coconut rice or even just some steamed basmati it's also a standalone meal. It's worth seeking out fresh turmeric for this, as it makes such a difference to the finished dish.

EGG, TOMATO & SPINACH CURRY WITH GINGER & TURMERIC

8 extra-large eggs

100 ml extra-virgin olive oil

2 large red onions, sliced into half-moons

5 garlic cloves, sliced

80 g ginger, julienned

8-cm piece of turmeric, finely grated (or 2 teaspoons ground turmeric)

2 bird's eye chillies, split lengthways

2 tablespoons yellow mustard seeds

2 teaspoons cumin seeds

2 teaspoons ground coriander

4 large handfuls of baby spinach leaves

1 tablespoon tomato paste

1 x 400 g can diced tomatoes

2 teaspoons salt flakes

300 ml vegetable or chicken stock (or water)

200 g natural yoghurt

1 bunch of coriander, leaves picked and roughly chopped

1 handful of cashews, toasted

1 lemon

steamed rice or Baked Coconut & Lemon Rice (page 186), to serve

Carefully lower the eggs into a saucepan of simmering water and cook for 5 ½ minutes. Refresh in cold water for 5 minutes and peel.

Heat the oil in a wide-based saucepan over medium heat. Add the onion, garlic, ginger, turmeric and chilli and cook for 10 minutes until softened. Add the mustard seeds, cumin seeds and ground coriander and cook for 1 minute. Add the spinach and cook for 4 minutes, stirring frequently. Add the tomato paste, tomato and salt, stir through and bring to a simmer. Add the stock and simmer for 5 minutes. Add the eggs and simmer for 5 minutes. Adjust the seasoning if necessary.

To serve, dollop on the yoghurt, sprinkle over the coriander and cashews and squeeze over the lemon. Serve with steamed rice or coconut rice on the side.

SERVES 4

TURMERIC

Turmeric, a rhizome in the ginger family, is native to southern India and its saffron hue and earthy spiciness are inseparable from Indian cuisine. Turmeric is either used fresh, or dried and ground into a powder, though it really is worth seeking out the fresh version. It's usually available at Asian grocers, and the aroma and vibrant colour is hard to beat. In addition to its culinary uses, turmeric is thought to have anti-inflammatory and cancer fighting properties, as well as helping to boost the immune system. Make up a tea of chopped turmeric and ginger infused in boiling water (with lemon and honey being optional extras) to soothe a sore throat or fight off any wintery ailments.

*I have great affection for a good fish curry, and I particularly like the Goan versions that are soured with tamarind. This recipe is not traditional as such, rather a mix of all the things that I love in a fish curry: tamarind, of course, tomato, okra, plenty of mustard seeds, beautifully fresh fish and the smoky fragrant aroma of curry leaves. It's worth tracking down fresh curry leaves at an Asian grocer, you can buy dried leaves, but they don't have the same intoxicating smoky charm. The fresh leaves also don't freeze terribly well, but will keep reasonably well stored in the crisper in a ziplock bag with most of the air removed. The coconut rice is perfect with this, but it also partners beautifully with my **Egg, Tomato & Spinach Curry** on page 184.*

SOUR FISH & OKRA CURRY WITH BAKED COCONUT & LEMON RICE

5 small garlic cloves

6-cm piece of ginger

6 roma tomatoes, roughly chopped

1 teaspoon freshly ground black pepper

1 tablespoon brown mustard seeds

2 teaspoons coriander seeds

2 tablespoons coconut oil

20 okra

2 teaspoons cumin seeds

1½ white onions, finely sliced

4 green bird's eye chillies, split lengthways

1 tablespoon salt flakes

3 tablespoons tamarind paste

1 x 1–1.2 kg blue-eye trevalla fillet, skin on, cut into 8 even portions

20 fresh curry leaves, on the stem

BAKED COCONUT & LEMON RICE

750 ml chicken or vegetable stock, hot

300 g basmati rice, soaked in cold water for 30 minutes and drained

60 g shredded coconut

1 tablespoon coconut oil

1 strip of lemon peel

1 teaspoon salt flakes

Preheat the oven to 160°C fan-forced (180°C conventional).

For the baked rice, add all the ingredients to a ceramic baking dish and stir to combine. Cover the rice with a piece of baking paper, making sure that the paper is touching the top of the rice (this will ensure that the liquid evaporates slowly). Bake for 30–40 minutes until the rice is cooked.

Meanwhile, for the curry, add the garlic, ginger, tomato, pepper and half the mustard and coriander seeds to a blender and puree until smooth.

Heat the oil in a wide-based saucepan over medium heat. Add the okra and cook for 3 minutes while stirring. Remove the okra from the pan and set aside.

Add the cumin and the remaining mustard and coriander seeds to the pan and fry until the mustard seeds pop. Add the onion and cook until starting to turn golden, about 5 minutes. Add the tomato mix, chilli and salt and bring to a simmer. Add the tamarind paste and 400 ml of water, reduce the heat and cook for 5 minutes. Return the okra to the pan and cook for 5 minutes. Tuck the fish into the sauce along with the curry leaves, cover and cook for 10 minutes over low heat. Adjust the seasoning if necessary and serve with the baked rice on the side.

SERVES 4–6

OKRA

My grandmother introduced me to okra with a simple lamb braise, which she finished with cumin and lemon, and I've been a fan ever since. It's great in stir-fries, curries and as a standalone vegetable, braised or fried. And it's just brilliant paired with tomato. Okra also works very well with an agrodolce (sweet and sour) dressing and a hint of allspice. It pops up in dishes across Africa and Asia, but is perhaps best known for its use in gumbo. Once cut or cooked for a long time, okra releases its characteristic sliminess – admittedly not for everyone – and is one of the methods used in conjunction with a roux, or on its own, to thicken the sauce. If you cook the okra for shorter periods or keep them whole, the slimy side that some people struggle with is easily avoided.

Rogan josh is a traditional Kashmiri lamb curry, probably arriving there, in one form or another, via Persia. It's incredibly popular all around the world, and is made in countless variations. This version uses lamb shoulder, which helps to enrich the sauce as the connective tissue breaks down during cooking. I've used the fairly traditional spicing elements of cassia, bay leaves, cloves and cardamom, with the heat and colour coming from Kashmiri chillies and turmeric. To get an even deeper red colour, as is traditional, add more of the chillies, just deseed them first. Don't skip the raita – it's not exactly traditional but it adds real freshness and a crisp raw contrast to the rich curry. Serve this with steamed basmati and **Naan** *(page 86)*

ROGAN JOSH

3 tablepoons ghee

3 red onions, sliced

2 fresh bay leaves

10 cloves

8 green cardamom pods, crushed

8-cm piece of cassia bark

1½ tablespoons fennel seeds

10-cm piece of ginger, finely julienned

6 garlic cloves, finely chopped

8-cm piece of turmeric, finely grated (or 2 teaspoons ground turmeric)

2 tablespoons ground coriander

2 teaspoons ground ginger

2 teaspoons Kashmiri chilli powder

6 large tomatoes, diced

1 tablespoon tomato paste

2 dried Kashmiri chillies

1½ tablespoons salt flakes

1.2 kg diced lamb shoulder

Naan (page 86), to serve

RAITA

1 red onion, finely sliced

4-cm piece of ginger, finely diced

2 handfuls of coriander leaves, chopped

juice of ½ lemon or lime

3 tablespoons thick natural yoghurt

2 pinches of salt flakes

2 teaspoons nigella seeds

Add the ghee to a wide-based saucepan over medium heat and fry the onion until turning golden, about 10 minutes. Add the bay leaves, cloves, cardamom, cassia and fennel seeds and fry for 2 minutes while stirring. Add the julienned ginger, the garlic and turmeric and cook for 1 minute. Add the ground coriander, ground ginger and chilli powder and stir through briefly until fragrant. Add a splash of water to cool the spices, then add the tomato, tomato paste, chillies and salt and stir through until combined. Add the lamb and stir through well to coat. Add 500 ml of water and bring to a simmer. Reduce the heat to low, cover the pan and cook for 45–60 minutes until the meat is tender. Adjust the seasoning and reduce the sauce a little if necessary.

For the raita, add all the ingredients to a medium bowl and combine.

Serve the curry with basmati rice, naan and the raita on the side.

SERVES 8

MY PAST

OLD-SCHOOL DISHES REINVENTED

STUPENDOUSLY GOOD GARLIC BREAD

**CHICKEN & CORN SOUP
WITH BROKEN VERMICELLI**

FRENCH FISH SOUP WITH SPICY ROUILLE

VIETNAMESE-STYLE STEAK TARTARE

CHICKEN LIVER PARFAIT

**MACARONI & CHEESE WITH MUSTARD
& FRESH TRUFFLE**

**PORK SCHNITZEL WITH BUFFALO
MOZZARELLA & FENNEL, APPLE & SOUR
CREAM SLAW**

AUTHENTIC PASTA CARBONARA

SAUSAGE RAGU WITH PAPPARDELLE

**TIERED SPONGE CAKE WITH RASPBERRY JAM
& WHIPPED CREAM**

**VANILLA AND FIG LEAF PANNA COTTA WITH
SCORCHED LEMON SYRUP & FRESH FIG**

DARK CHOCOLATE CREAM

You couldn't walk in to a restaurant in the eighties, Italian or otherwise, without stumbling over garlic bread. And then it was shunned for such a long time, becoming a daggy opening line for a menu, but there's no need to throw out what is a sound idea because it was done so badly so very often. Which is hard to understand really, especially when all you need is good bread, good butter, fresh garlic and parsley and a little seasoning. This version has a few more tweaks to it, but the principle is the same. If you only need one loaf, roll the leftover butter in baking paper and foil and freeze for another time.

STUPENDOUSLY GOOD GARLIC BREAD

6 garlic cloves

300 g unsalted butter, softened

2 teaspoons white miso paste

2 tablespoons finely grated Grana Padano

½ bunch of flat-leaf parsley, leaves picked and finely chopped

3 tablespoons extra-virgin olive oil

1 tablespoon salt flakes

20 grinds of black pepper

½ teaspoon cayenne pepper

2 loaves of white sourdough bread

Preheat the oven to 180°C fan-forced (200°C conventional).

Finely grate the garlic into a medium bowl. Add the butter, miso, Grana Padano, parsley, oil, salt, black pepper and cayenne and combine well.

Slice the loaves most of the way through in conventional slices, or both lengthways and across the loaf to make thick garlicky chunks. Butter the inside of the loaves generously with the garlic butter and wrap in foil. Bake for 15 minutes. Unwrap the foil slightly to just expose the top of the bread and bake for a further 5 minutes to crisp up the crust and serve immediately.

MAKES 2 LOAVES

GARLIC

There is actually a bewildering array of garlic cultivars grown around the world, probably (according to the incredibly informative australiangarlic.net.au website) numbering over a thousand. To the untrained eye, most Australian garlic looks pretty much the same, perhaps some bulbs have more pink or red tones, some with larger or more compact cloves, and some hotter on the palate or more pungent than others, but more or less similar. And although the subtle differences are really pretty interesting for the garlic obsessed, for most people this kind of detail is too much information. What is important, though, is making sure the garlic you are using has been grown and stored correctly.

Australian garlic is typically of very high quality and, if dried properly and stored cool and dry, will last well. When not available, imports from places such as Mexico and Argentina can be good substitutes, but I never buy the ultra-white garlic bulbs from China, and under no circumstances would I ever, ever buy garlic in a jar. Chinese garlic has often been chemically treated to increase its shelf life and the brilliant white skin has more to do with chlorine bleach than variety. When selecting garlic, choose bulbs that are firm when squeezed, and make sure that there are no green sprouts emerging from the top of the cloves. Also, pull back some of the skin and smell the cloves – if they are at all musty or damp smelling, choose another bulb.

Chicken and corn soup was such a staple in Chinese restaurants when I was growing up. As a family, we'd always order it when we went to the Oriental Jade restaurant in Greensborough, along with prawn toast, spring rolls, chicken and cashew stir-fry, beef in black bean, special fried rice and lemon chicken, and dad would always lash out with the sizzling Mongolian beef. All topped off with a round of deep-fried ice cream and a handful, if we were lucky, of fortune cookies. Perhaps not the most authentic Chinese cuisine, but it made us pretty happy. The only jarring note was the Saturday night feature of an electric organist. A much younger me – old enough to know better, mind you – put a stop to the proceedings one night by pulling the plug on the keyboard. It sighed sadly into silence as the whole restaurant turned to stare at me, plug in hand. No more Oriental Jade for me.

*I still love spring rolls and prawn toast – reinvented, of course – and this version of chicken and corn soup makes me very happy. I've kept the principle the same, but I just use the best and freshest ingredients I can find. Try this with **Chicken Bone Broth** (page 52) for an even more intense and nourishing soup.*

CHICKEN & CORN SOUP WITH BROKEN VERMICELLI

150 g rice vermicelli

3 chicken thigh fillets

2 tablespoons grapeseed oil (or other neutral oil)

salt flakes and ground white pepper

2 litres chicken stock or Chicken Bone Broth (page 52)

3 garlic cloves, finely chopped

6-cm piece of ginger, finely grated

4 corn cobs, kernels sliced off

1½ tablespoons cornflour dissolved in 2 tablespoons water

3 eggs, lightly beaten

4 spring onions, finely sliced

soy sauce, to serve

sesame oil, to serve

Soak the noodles in boiling water until soft. Drain, snip into short lengths and set aside.

Coat the chicken in a little oil, season with salt and pepper and seal well in a hot frying pan.

Bring the stock to a simmer in a medium saucepan. Add the chicken and cook until very tender, about 25 minutes. Remove the chicken from the stock and shred the meat. Turn the heat off and set the stock aside.

Heat the remaining oil in a large, wide-based saucepan over medium heat. Add the garlic and ginger and cook for 1–2 minutes. Add the corn, season and stir through. Add the stock, 500 ml of water and the shredded chicken and bring to a simmer. Add the noodles and simmer for 3 minutes. Start whisking the soup before adding the cornflour slurry. Keep whisking until the soup thickens, about 2 minutes. Add the beaten egg and spring onion and stir to distribute evenly. Bring just to a simmer and turn off the heat.

Serve the soup with soy sauce and sesame oil on the side to season as required.

SERVES 8–10

6 whole green prawns

1 kg whole gurnard (or sand or grey mullet), filleted, skin left on and bones reserved

100 ml extra-virgin olive oil

1 onion, finely sliced

3 celery stalks, finely sliced

1 fennel bulb, finely sliced

1 leek, white and pale green parts only, finely sliced

5 garlic cloves, sliced

1 teaspoon fennel seeds

2 pinches of saffron threads

1 fresh bay leaf

4 thyme sprigs

finely grated zest of ½ orange and juice of 1 orange

½ long red chilli, chopped

3 tablespoons tomato paste

1 tablespoon white miso paste

3 tablespoons Pernod or another pastis

200 g canned diced tomatoes

grilled chunks of sourdough, to serve

SPICY ROUILLE

2 red capsicums

250 ml extra-virgin olive oil, plus extra

30 g sourdough bread, no crusts

3 garlic cloves

2 bird's eye chillies, finely chopped

3 teaspoons tomato paste

2 teaspoons ground coriander

1 pinch of saffron threads

2 teaspoons caster sugar

1 teaspoon salt flakes

2 extra-large egg yolks

Many years ago, my paternal grandmother, or meme, used to make a fish soup laced with orange, saffron, tomato and anise – a French soup seen through her Tunisian filter. Hers was rustic with big chunks of fish through it, rather than the puree that is more common in French bistros, although the flavours are much the same. On the occasions that I've been to France, I have always sought out a version of this in a traditional brasserie, and it has always brought back a flood of memories.

You can also add some steamed mussels or clams to the finished soup, just make sure you serve it piping hot with plenty of good bread. Leftover rouille is brilliant on toast with some goat's curd or mature goat's cheese, on eggs, in a rare roast beef sandwich, or with pan-fried sardines or grilled tuna.

FRENCH FISH SOUP WITH SPICY ROUILLE

Preheat the oven to 180°C fan-forced (200°C conventional).

Remove the heads from the prawns, peel and devein. Add the heads and shells to a medium saucepan.

Rinse the fish bones well, making sure to remove any traces of blood from the head, and add to the pan with the prawn trimmings. You can add some aromatic vegetables here if you like, or some of the trimmings from the vegetables for the soup, but it's not absolutely necessary, as you'll get plenty of flavour when you make the soup. Cover with 3 litres of water and bring to a gentle simmer. Skim off any impurities and simmer very gently for 20 minutes. Strain and set aside.

For the soup, heat the oil in a large, wide-based saucepan over low–medium heat. Add the onion, celery, fennel, leek and garlic and cook, stirring frequently, for 15 minutes until softened but not coloured. Add the fennel seeds, saffron, bay leaf, thyme, orange zest, chilli, tomato paste and miso and stir through for 1–2 minutes. Stir through the fish and prawns, add the orange juice and pastis and bring to a simmer. Add the tomatoes and 2.5 litres of the stock and simmer for 40 minutes.

Meanwhile, for the rouille, lightly coat the capsicums with a little extra oil and roast on a baking tray for 30 minutes. Cool slightly, slip the skins off, core and deseed.

Soak the bread in water for 5 minutes. Drain and squeeze out the liquid in your hands.

Add the capsicum, garlic, chilli, tomato paste, coriander, saffron, sugar and salt to a blender or food processor and blitz. Add the

bread and egg yolks and blitz until smooth. With the motor running, drizzle in 250 ml of oil in a steady stream until incorporated and emulsified. Leftover rouille will keep for 10 days in the refrigerator.

Once the soup is cooked, remove the bay leaf and thyme and blitz with a hand-held blender. Pass through a coarse sieve and adjust the seasoning.

Serve the soup with the rouille and plenty of grilled bread on the side.

SERVES 8–10

Steak tartare is one of those old-fashioned French dishes — and one that featured heavily in my early years as an apprentice chef — that really polarises people. You don't get too many lukewarm responses from people when you serve them raw meat with raw egg yolks on top. I do love a good steak tartare, and by good I mean beautiful quality meat that has been cut to order and mixed with the best egg yolks and a deft addition of seasoning.

Given the French influence on Vietnamese cuisine, it makes perfect sense to give a classic steak tartare a South-East Asian makeover. This dish is so suited to hot weather, and the punchy, fragrant flavours and burst of heat are a great complement to the chilled meat. You could also serve the tartare in witlof leaves as elegant finger food.

600 g eye fillet
1 small garlic clove, finely grated
2 red shallots, very finely chopped
2 lemongrass stalks, white part only, very finely sliced
4 hot Thai chillies, very finely sliced
1 tablespoon Dijon mustard
1½ tablespoons fish sauce
2½ tablespoons extra-virgin olive oil
1½ teaspoons freshly ground black pepper
salt flakes
3 egg yolks
2 limes, peeled and segmented
2 kaffir lime leaves, very finely shredded
2 tablespoons ground toasted rice
1 handful of coriander leaves
prawn crackers, to serve
½ iceberg lettuce, separated into cups
½ bunch of Vietnamese mint
1 celery heart, leaves only (optional)

DRESSING

2½ tablespoons fish sauce
2½ tablespoons extra-virgin olive oil
juice of 1 lime
1 hot Thai chilli, very finely sliced (optional)

VIETNAMESE-STYLE STEAK TARTARE

Finely dice the beef as evenly as possible — take your time doing this, as it improves the presentation dramatically. Refrigerate until chilled, but don't do this too far ahead of time or the meat will oxidise.

Add the beef, garlic, shallots, half the lemongrass, half the chilli, the mustard, fish sauce, oil and pepper to a large bowl, season with salt to taste and combine gently.

To make the dressing, combine all the ingredients in a small bowl or jug.

Pile the tartare onto a serving platter and top with the egg yolks. Scatter over the lime segments, lime leaves, ground rice, coriander and remaining chilli and lemongrass. Pile up the prawn crackers on one side of the platter and the lettuce cups, Vietnamese mint and celery leaves on the other.

Mix the egg yolks through at the table and serve the dressing on the side. Your guests can assemble the elements in the lettuce cups or on the prawn crackers as they like, or eat the tartare as is and nibble on the lettuce and crackers for a bit of textural contrast.

SERVES 6

Pâté was just so popular in the seventies and eighties, and I remember eating it, and liking it, even as a little kid. Back then, sealing the pâté in a fluted ramekin with a layer of port wine jelly was de rigueur, *and if it didn't come with curled-up bits of melba toast, or at least the little squares from a packet, you weren't doing it properly. This silky parfait (meaning 'perfect' in French and, in this context, essentially a super-smooth pâté) has evolved out of a recipe from my very early days of professional training, even before I was schooled in classical French technique at Tansy's. The spicing in this is quite traditional, but I've upped the quantities a bit to suit my palate.*

Ensure that the livers you use are sparklingly fresh, and seek out organic ones if you can. Serve the parfait with **Red Onion & Sherry Jam** *(page 32), cornichons and baguette or* **Brioche** *(pages 92–3), and it's great in a* **Bánh Mì** *(pages 146–7). This recipe can be doubled.*

CHICKEN LIVER PARFAIT

400 g chicken livers
500 ml milk
300 g butter
1 fresh bay leaf
4 thyme sprigs
3 French shallots, finely diced
2 garlic cloves, chopped
extra-virgin olive oil
180 ml brandy
½ teaspoon ground white pepper
¼ nutmeg, finely grated
¼ teaspoon Chinese five-spice
salt flakes
3 tablespoons cream (35% fat)

This recipe will need to be started the day before serving.

Add the livers and milk to a bowl, cover and refrigerate overnight.

The next day, drain the livers and dry well on paper towel. Trim off any connective tissue and discard.

Dice 75 g of butter and set aside at room temperature. Melt another 75 g of butter in a small saucepan with the bay leaf and thyme and set aside to infuse.

Sweat the shallots and garlic in a medium saucepan with a little oil until softened. Add half the brandy and reduce until sticky. Take off the heat and set aside.

Combine the white pepper, nutmeg and five-spice in a small bowl.

Heat a large frying pan over high heat until quite hot. Lightly oil the livers and sear quickly in two batches, seasoning well with salt as you go. After 1 minute, flip the livers and add half the diced butter and half the spice mix. Once the other side is seared, deglaze with half the remaining brandy and immediately remove the livers from the pan – they should still be rare. Boil the brandy for 20 seconds and pour the juices into the pan with the shallots. Wipe out the frying pan and repeat for the remaining livers.

Add the livers and the shallot mix to a blender and puree. Remove the herbs from the melted butter and gradually add to the blender along with the cream. Once smooth, adjust the seasoning if necessary and pass through a very fine sieve. Divide the parfait between ramekins or jars.

Gently melt the remaining butter in a small saucepan until the solids sink to the bottom of the pan. Stand for 5 minutes off the

heat before spooning the liquid into a small jug. Pour the clarified butter on top of each parfait, cover with plastic wrap and set in the refrigerator – this process will seal and preserve the parfait. Use within 5 days.

MAKES 3–4 SMALL POTS

When I was growing up, macaroni and cheese was one of those midweek dinner dishes that was both easy for mum to prepare and kept us kids pretty quiet … well, maybe not quiet, but happy. Mind you, that version never had fresh truffle on it. I've certainly taken this in a different and totally luxurious direction. This is a great weekend indulgence, especially if you take the American steakhouse route and pair it with some thick barbecued steaks (try it with my **Bistecca alla Fiorentina** on page 240) – maybe just whip up a little salad as well.

MACARONI & CHEESE WITH MUSTARD & FRESH TRUFFLE

500 g macaroni or rigatoni

1 litre milk

1 fresh bay leaf

90 g butter

4 garlic cloves, finely sliced

1 white onion, finely diced

salt flakes and freshly ground black pepper

1 teaspoon curry powder

90 g plain flour

200 ml cream (35% fat)

2 tablespoons Dijon mustard

120 g vintage cheddar, grated

100 g Grana Padano, finely grated

2 handfuls of fresh breadcrumbs

15 g fresh truffle

Preheat the oven to 180°C fan-forced (200°C conventional).

Cook the pasta in plenty of boiling salted water until al dente.

While the pasta cooks, add the milk and bay leaf to a small saucepan and heat without boiling.

Melt the butter in a medium saucepan over medium heat. Add the garlic and onion, season and cook for about 4 minutes until fragrant and softened. Add the curry powder and stir through briefly. Add the flour and stir for a minute or so to cook out the raw flavour. Pour in the hot milk and cook for about 2 minutes while whisking constantly until thickened and smooth. Add the cream, mustard, cheddar and half the parmesan and whisk until combined, season and tip into a large bowl.

Add the cooked pasta to the sauce and stir through until combined. Tip the pasta mix into a ceramic baking dish, top with the extra Grana Padano and the breadcrumbs and bake for 20–30 minutes until golden and bubbling.

Shave the truffle over the hot pasta and serve.

SERVES 4–6

TRUFFLES

There's no getting past the fact that truffles are frighteningly expensive. And even though you'd only ever use a tiny amount, they're, well, still frighteningly expensive. They are amazing, though, and well worth indulging in for a treat, just make sure you get what you pay for. A truffle should have an intense aroma, and much more so when cut and gently warmed on a finished dish. When selecting a truffle always smell it first, if there is little or no aroma, don't waste your money. When at their best, Australian truffles are very much the equal of the imported ones.

*Mum used to make pretty good schnitzels when I was a kid; she still does. They were usually chicken, though sometimes veal, and almost always with potato mash and roasted peppers. These days, I prefer a fresher side dish to balance the richness of the schnitzel, and this crunchy slaw does the job perfectly. The slaw would also be great with a steak (try my **Bistecca alla Fiorentina** on page 240).*

PORK SCHNITZEL WITH BUFFALO MOZZARELLA & FENNEL, APPLE & SOUR CREAM SLAW

4 × 180 g trimmed pork loin fillets, beaten out to just under 5 mm thick

75 g plain flour

2 eggs, beaten

100 g panko or fresh white breadcrumbs

100 ml olive oil

2 large balls of buffalo mozzarella, cut into 2-mm thick slices

lemon wedges, to serve

FENNEL & APPLE SLAW

1 large fennel bulb, very finely sliced, fronds picked

1 large granny smith apple, skin on, julienned

½ celeriac, trimmed and julienned

4 mint sprigs, leaves picked

2 long green chillies, finely sliced

1 red shallot, finely diced

2 tablespoons finely grated Parmigiano-Reggiano

DRESSING

3 tablespoons extra-virgin olive oil

2 tablespoons sour cream

1 tablespoon sherry vinegar

salt flakes and freshly ground black pepper

For the dressing, add all the ingredients to a small bowl, season and combine.

For the slaw, combine all the ingredients in a large bowl and add the dressing. Mix well with your hands and set aside for 10 minutes before serving.

Preheat the oven grill on high.

Coat the pork fillets with flour, dust off any excess, then dip in the beaten egg and finally coat well with the panko or breadcrumbs.

Heat the oil in a large frying pan over high heat and cook the schnitzels for about 1½ minutes on each side until golden. Transfer to a baking tray, top with the mozzarella and flash in the oven for 1 minute to soften the cheese slightly.

Serve the schnitzels with the slaw and lemon wedges on the side.

SERVES 4

PORK

Sadly, like chickens (see page 145), pigs are easy targets for factory farming. They can be raised in limited space and the economics of doing so are sometimes a competitive necessity for farmers. But the increase in demand for ethical meat products has seen a real demand for pork that has been reared sympathetically. Free-range pork is more expensive, but the meat is so much better and the moral equation has a lot more balance. Free-range pork producers often specialise in rare breeds, ones that typically have a good (and delicious) layer of fat and a deeper flavour profile. And if you're concerned about depleting the stocks of rare breeds, don't be. Ethical commercial farming is the only way they won't disappear – perversely their only lifeline – having been abandoned by conventional farmers many years ago.

Unless you're slow cooking the fattier parts until meltingly tender, pork doesn't need to be cooked through. Convention has always dictated that pork needs to be cooked completely, but this just isn't the case. Pork cuts that don't have much fat, like those of many other animals, really benefit from being cooked just enough to still retain a good blush of pink. This may be a bit confronting for people who have been repeatedly told the opposite, but trust me, the difference is amazing.

FENNEL

Bulb or Florence fennel is one of my absolute favourite vegetables. As a kid, I would happily snack on it raw, pinching it from the kitchen bench while mum cooked. It was also rampant in my grandmother's garden, and she used the fronds as thoughtfully as the bulbs. I have a vivid memory of her chopping big handfuls and mixing them with lamb mince to make gorgeously scented skinless sausages.

Although available in the markets year round, late autumn and winter is when fennel is at its sweet and crunchy best. Pick unblemished fat bulbs with vibrant green fronds still attached – not only are they a pretty, anise-tinged soft herb, but they also indicate the freshness of the bulb. Also, don't be tempted by the flat, fan-shaped versions, they tend to be stringy and lack any delicacy of flavour.

The first spaghetti 'carbonara' I ever ate was on Lygon Street back in the … let's just say it was the eighties. A massive bowl of pasta swimming in cream with plenty of bacon, sliced button mushrooms and the unmistakable aroma of jarred garlic. I wouldn't say I minded it much back then, but, over the years, I realised I could definitely do better. Firstly, out with the mushrooms, in with fresh garlic and a lighter hand with the cream. A bit later, the bacon or pancetta had to be the best I could get, as did the pasta, and it had to be al dente. Later came a little dried chilli, and the cream faded to a trickle to subtly enrich the golden egg yolks. Today, it is far more authentic. No cream, just the most luscious organic yolks, the best oil and the best cheese (Parmigiano-Reggiano – indulgent, I know). Simple and just so beautiful. I cooked this version for my mother one day. Her response? 'This isn't carbonara! Where are the mushrooms?' Sometimes you just can't win. To fully redeem that old memory, try this with my **Garlic Bread** *(page 194).*

AUTHENTIC PASTA CARBONARA

500 g strozzapreti (or quality pasta of your choice)

6 extra-large egg yolks

120 ml extra-virgin olive oil

salt flakes and freshly ground black pepper

10 thick slices of pancetta (or dry-cured bacon), cut into lardons

4 garlic cloves, finely sliced

150 g Parmigiano-Reggiano, finely grated

chilli flakes, to serve

Cook the pasta in plenty of boiling salted water until al dente.

Meanwhile, lightly beat the egg yolks, 2 tablespoons of the oil and a pinch of salt in a medium bowl.

Add the remaining oil to a large frying pan over medium heat and fry the pancetta until crisp, about 5 minutes – don't worry about this being oily, it's integral to building the sauce. Add the garlic and fry for a minute or so until lightly golden and fragrant. Lift the cooked pasta directly from the pot into the pan, season with salt and pepper, toss to combine and take off the heat.

Tip the yolk mix into the pan and immediately toss through until evenly coated. Add a handful of Parmigiano-Reggiano and toss through quickly. Divide the pasta between serving bowls, sprinkle over some chilli flakes and serve with the remaining Parmigiano-Reggiano on the side.

SERVES 4

*Dad was the bolognaise maker in our family house. Like many dads back then, that was his one dish. This, however, is not his recipe. Sorry, Dad. I cook many different versions of a meat ragu, and usually have one on the go ready to toss with pasta, layer into a lasagne, fill a **Jaffle** (page 64) or an **Empanada** (page 133), and for many other things too. This one is so easy to make and you get such a flavour punch from the sausages, as they've been seasoned and lightly cured already. This is delicious when it has just been made, but a ragu always improves over a day or so.*

SAUSAGE RAGU WITH PAPPARDELLE

3 tablespoons extra-virgin olive oil

150 g thickly cut pancetta, diced

750 g pork and fennel sausages, casings removed

2 onions, diced

6 garlic cloves, finely chopped

1 carrot, finely diced

3 celery stalks, finely sliced

2 fresh bay leaves

½ teaspoon chilli flakes

2 teaspoons fennel seeds

2 tablespoons tomato paste

400 ml red wine

500 ml chicken stock

2 × 400 g cans diced tomatoes

3 rosemary sprigs

2 oregano sprigs, leaves picked

salt flakes and freshly ground black pepper

100 g pappardelle per person

finely grated Grana Padano, to serve

Heat a heavy-based saucepan over medium heat. Add half the oil and the pancetta and crumble in the sausage meat. Fry, stirring every few minutes, until the meat is golden brown. Add the onion, garlic, carrot, celery, bay leaves, chilli flakes and fennel seeds and stir well – the vegetables will sweat a little and effectively deglaze the pan. Cook gently for 15 minutes, stirring every now and then, until the vegetables are soft and slightly caramelised. Add the tomato paste and red wine and bring to a simmer. Add the stock, tomatoes, rosemary and oregano and continue to simmer for about 45 minutes over low heat until the ragu is thick and intensely flavoured. Adjust the seasoning and stir through the remaining oil.

To serve, cook the pasta according to the packet instructions and toss through the ragu in the pan. Take the pan directly to the table and serve with plenty of Grana Padano on the side.

SERVES 6–8

During my childhood, at the slightest sniff of an occasion sponge cakes would magically appear. Mum made a good sponge, but her mum was the real expert, her wares regularly lining trestle tables at church and school fetes. It was also the essential dessert – along with lemon tart and chocolate cake – in restaurants when I did my apprenticeship. I think I probably overdid the sponge cakes back then, and they fell right out of my repertoire for a long time. But a good sponge layered with some homemade jam and freshly whipped cream can really be a thing of beauty, and is well worth revisiting. This recipe produces a slightly stronger crumb than some other recipes, but it's almost foolproof, taking the temperature vagaries of domestic ovens in its stride.

TIERED SPONGE CAKE WITH RASPBERRY JAM & WHIPPED CREAM

180 g self-raising flour

½ teaspoon baking powder

1 teaspoon custard powder

6 extra-large eggs

185 g caster sugar

40 g unsalted butter, melted

180 g Simple Roasted Raspberry Jam (page 14)

350 ml thickened cream, whipped

icing sugar, to serve

Preheat the oven to 185°C fan-forced (205°C conventional). Grease two 16-cm springform cake tins and line with baking paper.

Sift the flour, baking powder and custard powder into a medium bowl.

Add the eggs to the bowl of a stand mixer and whisk until foaming. Gradually rain in the sugar while mixing until thick. Fold in the dry mix by hand, and then fold in the melted butter. Pour into the prepared tins and bake for 20–25 minutes until springy to the touch. Set aside for 5 minutes before turning out onto a wire rack.

Carefully slice the cooled sponges in half horizontally. Layer the base of one sponge with a third of the jam and cream and top with the other half. Top with another third of the jam and cream, then the other base, followed by the remaining jam and cream, and finally the last layer of sponge. Dust with icing sugar and serve.

SERVES 8

I hate to think how many panna cottas I've made in my life. Over the last couple of decades at the Melbourne Wine Room, Icebergs and mr. wolf, I've worked with Italian-focused food, and if one version of panna cotta ever came off any of the menus it was replaced with another one before long. This recipe is a relatively recent development, using fig leaves to scent the cream and a scorched lemon syrup to add a marmalade tang as a counterpoint to the creamy sweetness. Fig leaves are so full of the same smoky scent that figs carry and will infuse into warm liquid quite readily. Even the leaves from my (sadly) ornamental fig tree work well.

VANILLA AND FIG LEAF PANNA COTTA WITH SCORCHED LEMON SYRUP & FRESH FIG

3 ½ leaves gold-strength gelatine
370 ml milk
750 ml cream (35% fat)
120 g caster sugar
½ vanilla bean, split lengthways, seeds scraped
5 small freshly picked fig leaves
10 slices of ripe fig

SCORCHED LEMON SYRUP
250 g caster sugar
finely grated zest and juice of 5 lemons (about 350 ml)

For the syrup, add the sugar to a medium saucepan and place over high heat. Shake the pan frequently so that the sugar liquefies and colours evenly, but don't stir. Continue to caramelise the sugar, shaking the pan when necessary, for around 8 minutes. You want a quite darkly coloured caramel, which will give the sauce a light bitterness, but make sure it doesn't burn. Remove from the heat and immediately add the lemon zest and juice – stand back, as it will spit. Stir, return to the heat and bring to a simmer. Once fully incorporated, take off the heat and pour into a jar or jug. Refrigerate until cold and syrupy.

Add the gelatine to a bowl or jug of cold water and set aside for 5 minutes.

Warm the milk, cream, sugar and vanilla bean and seeds in a medium saucepan over medium heat. Roll up the fig leaves to break the fibres, which will release the flavour, and add to the pan. Bring up to a simmer and take off the heat.

Lift the gelatine from the water, squeezing out any excess in your hands, and add to the pan. Stir until dissolved and set aside for 15 minutes for the flavours to infuse.

Strain the mix through a fine strainer and pour into ten small glasses or jars. Refrigerate for at least 6 hours, or preferably overnight.

To serve, pour 1½ tablespoons of the syrup onto each panna cotta and place a fig slice on each.

MAKES 10

For me, there are few desserts quite as nostalgic as chocolate mousse – well, perhaps cassata, or a forbidden apple. It was to the eighties what lemon tart and sticky date pudding were to the nineties. Done well, there's no need for something like chocolate mousse to fall out of favour, but plenty of junket-like commercial versions left a bad taste in the collective mouth – yes, literally. This recipe isn't really a classic chocolate mousse, it's that bit denser and more deeply flavoured. Like taking pure chocolate and making it smooth, creamy and just that little bit richer – all good things.

*You could add a spike of your favourite liqueur to this, or even some cardamom or cloves. Stirring some chopped chocolate through the mix would add a nice textural foil, as would chopped savoiardi biscuits. A scoop of this is delicious just as it is or with a slick of **Dulce de Leche** (page 154), but for an elegant individual dessert, set in small dishes or glasses and top with crushed praline.*

DARK CHOCOLATE CREAM

375 g quality dark chocolate (minimum 70% cocoa), chopped

75 g unsalted butter

1½ leaves gold-strength gelatine

450 ml cream (35% fat)

150 ml milk

3 extra-large egg yolks

75 g caster sugar

75 g glucose powder

½ teaspoon salt flakes

cocoa powder, for dusting

chocolate balls or grated or splintered chocolate, to serve

Dulce de Leche (page 154), to serve (optional)

Add the chocolate and butter to a large stainless steel bowl and place over a saucepan with a few centimetres of barely simmering water in it. Once mostly melted, stir through until incorporated and take off the heat.

Add the gelatine to a small jug or bowl of cold water and set aside for about 5 minutes.

Add 150 ml of the cream and the milk to a small saucepan, bring to a simmer and turn off the heat.

Add the egg yolks, sugar and glucose to a medium bowl and whisk until combined. Slowly add the warm cream mix while whisking constantly. Pour into a medium saucepan and cook over low heat while stirring constantly until thickened slightly, about 3–5 minutes. Take off the heat.

Squeeze the gelatine of excess water, add to the custard and stir until dissolved. Add the chocolate mix and the salt to the pan and stir until combined. Strain through a fine sieve into a large bowl and set aside to cool at room temperature.

Gently whip the remaining cream, fold through the cooled chocolate mix and transfer to a container. Cover and refrigerate until set, about 2 hours.

Spoon the chocolate cream into serving bowls and sprinkle with cocoa. Serve as is, or decorate with chocolate balls, or grated or splintered chocolate, and a slick of dulce de leche (if using).

SERVES 10–12

BIG GESTURES

SPECIAL FEASTS TO SHARE

ROASTED WHOLE SNAPPER WITH CORIANDER SALT, LEMON, BAY & GREEN HARISSA

FISHERMAN'S BASKET WITH NORI TARTARE

FRIED BRINED CHICKEN WITH CORN SLAW

BO SSAM

PULLED PORK BELLY WITH TORTILLAS, LIME & HERB SALSA & CHIPOTLE ADOBO

BISTECCA ALLA FIORENTINA

I have a real thing for fish cooked on the bone. I've almost always featured a whole fish on my menus, and I always look for one when I go out. Besides presenting beautifully, a whole fish yields such succulent and delectable meat, as it retains so much of its moisture. Cooking a large fish like this is ideal, as the flesh comes away easily in large pieces and it's easy to leave most of the bones behind. Only buy the freshest fish for this, one with crystal-clear eyes and firm flesh that smells of the sea – if you can't find any, have something else for dinner.

This harissa recipe makes more than you will need for the fish. I love having it in the fridge, and I always find ways of using it: dilute with a little vinaigrette and toss through shaved cabbage or freshly boiled potatoes; stir into yoghurt to go with a gozleme, haloumi pastry or just some warmed pide; drizzle over grilled lamb chops, sausages or sliced steak; toss through roasted carrots just prior to serving; stir into a soup or stew at the last minute; or drizzle over a fried egg and wrap in pita for a delicious breakfast on the run.

ROASTED WHOLE SNAPPER WITH CORIANDER SALT, LEMON, BAY & GREEN HARISSA

1 × 1.7–2 kg snapper, cleaned, scaled and scored

3 lemons, 1 whole and 2 sliced, plus extra wedges to serve

1½ tablespoons Coriander & Black Pepper Salt (page 26)

3 garlic cloves

1 orange, sliced

6 fresh bay leaves

2 tablespoons extra-virgin olive oil

HARISSA

2 teaspoons cumin seeds

2½ teaspoons caraway seeds

2 teaspoons coriander seeds

100 ml extra-virgin olive oil

200 g long green chillies (about 10)

100 g baby spinach leaves, chopped

3 handfuls of coriander leaves, chopped

1 tablespoon caster sugar

2 small garlic cloves, finely grated

2 teaspoons salt flakes

2½ tablespoons water

LEMON YOGHURT

300 g natural yoghurt

juice of ½ lemon

½ teaspoon salt flakes

Preheat the oven to 220°C fan-forced (240°C conventional).

For the harissa, toast the cumin, caraway and coriander seeds in a small frying pan until fragrant and lightly coloured, about 2 minutes. Grind to a powder using a mortar and pestle or spice grinder. Add the spices along with the remaining ingredients to a blender or food processor and blitz to a smooth paste. Refrigerate until needed. Leftover harissa will keep for 2–3 days in the refrigerator.

Score the skin of the fish on both sides halfway through the flesh and along the length of the spine. Make another incision on an angle across the back of the head – this will help the fish cook more evenly and also make the flesh easier to remove once cooked.

Lay out two lengths of foil so that they overlap in the middle. Place another piece down the middle covering the overlap. Top with two layers of baking paper and place the fish on top. Squeeze the whole lemon over the fish and inside the cavity. Season with the coriander salt, finely grate over the garlic, tuck the lemon slices, orange slices and bay leaves into the cavity and drizzle with the oil. Cover with baking paper and foil and roll the edges together to seal. Place on a baking tray and roast for 45 minutes.

Meanwhile, for the lemon yoghurt, combine all the ingredients in a small bowl and set aside.

Remove the fish from the oven and open the parcel. Return to the oven for 15 minutes until slightly coloured. Rest for 5 minutes, spooning the juices over the fish a few times, before serving.

Serve the fish with the harissa, lemon yoghurt and lemon wedges.

SERVES 6

Roasted Whole Snapper with Coriander Salt, Lemon, Bay & Green Harissa

Fisherman's Basket with Nori Tartare

Back in the early nineties, I took over the head chef role at a hotel called Haskin's, and while I was in the process of changing the bar menu I had to watch some pretty sad fisherman's baskets leave the kitchen. You know the ones, a miserable collection of 'seafood' coated in oil-sodden batter dumped in a cane basket lined with a red paper napkin. By the time I had finished with it, it was on the restaurant menu – but only as a special, because I'd made far too much work for myself in the process! This is such a beautifully crunchy batter and the nori tartare is really quite spectacular with it. Naturally, only use the brightest and best seafood for this.

oil, for deep-frying

6 shiso leaves

6 × 5-mm thick discs of sweet potato, blanched for 3 minutes, drained and set aside to dry

6 pieces of daikon from Spiced Chinese Pickles (page 46), drained

6 scallops

12 black mussels, steamed open, top shell removed

1 calamari, sliced into rings with wings attached, tentacles divided into pairs and cut into shorter lengths

6 green prawn cutlets, deveined

6 skinless flathead fillets, cut in half lengthways

Sichuan & Mandarin Salt (page 24), to serve

lemon wedges, to serve

NORI TARTARE

4 sheets of nori, hydrated in 80 ml of boiling water

250 g Mayonnaise (for a recipe, see page 31)

4 spring onions, white and pale green parts only, finely sliced

2 handfuls of dill fronds

3 tablespoons chopped gherkins or mixed Spiced Chinese Pickles (page 46)

1 tablespoon Dijon mustard

2 teaspoons umeboshi puree

1 teaspoon sesame oil

BEER BATTER

250 g plain flour, plus extra

250 g cornflour

1 tablespoon salt flakes

375 ml beer

350 ml sparkling mineral water

FISHERMAN'S BASKET WITH NORI TARTARE

For the tartare, drain the nori and slice very finely. Combine with the remaining ingredients and set aside.

Preheat the oven to 100°C conventional. Line two baking trays with a couple of layers of paper towel and place in the oven.

Preheat a deep-fryer or large saucepan of oil to 180°C.

For the batter, combine the flour, cornflour and salt in a large bowl and make a well in the centre. Combine the beer and mineral water in a jug and gradually add to the bowl while whisking until a smooth batter.

Batter and cook each batch of ingredients separately. Firstly dust in some extra plain flour, shake off any excess and drag through the batter. Allow the excess batter to drip off and then fry until golden – approximate timings: shiso 1 minute, sweet potato and daikon 1½ minutes, scallops 2 minutes, mussels and calamari 2½ minutes, prawns 3 minutes, and flathead 3–4 minutes. Immediately season with Sichuan salt and keep warm in the oven on the prepared trays while you cook the remaining items.

Arrange all the items on a serving platter and serve with the nori tartare, lemon wedges and extra Sichuan salt on the side.

SERVES 6

*This is seriously crunchy fried chicken scented with oregano and a subtle hint of spice. It's also incredibly succulent and moist – a pretty happy combination. Taking the time to brine the chicken really makes a big difference, it seasons the meat all the way through and helps to lock in the moisture while it cooks. This is a great recipe if you're entertaining, as it's easy to make a bigger batch and you can keep the cooked chicken warm in a low oven while you cook the next lot. If you're catering for a stand-up occasion, try just cooking drumsticks to make it even easier for your guests to handle. Leftover chicken comes up very well in a sandwich the next day, and if you want to add a little heat, try this with some **Gochujang Chilli Sauce** (page 40).*

FRIED BRINED CHICKEN WITH CORN SLAW

1 × 1.6 kg chicken, cut into 8 pieces

200–300 g cooking salt

oil, for deep-frying

150 g plain flour, plus extra

150 g tapioca flour

1½ tablespoons salt flakes

20 grinds of black pepper

2 tablespoons dried Greek oregano

2 tablespoons garlic powder

2 teaspoons ground turmeric

½ teaspoon curry powder

3 eggwhites, whisked

CORN SLAW

2½ tablespoons extra-virgin olive oil

1½ tablespoons white wine vinegar

2 teaspoons caster sugar

salt flakes and freshly ground black pepper

¼ white cabbage, finely shredded

3 corn cobs, simmered for 5 minutes in salted water, kernels sliced off

½ white onion, thinly sliced

80 g Parmigiano-Reggiano, finely grated

Allowing enough water to fully submerge the chicken pieces, make a brine solution by dissolving 100 g of cooking salt per litre of water in a large container or non-reactive saucepan. Place the chicken in the brine, ensuring that it is completely submerged, and refrigerate for 2–4 hours.

Remove the chicken from the brine and dry with paper towel.

Preheat a deep-fryer or large saucepan of oil to 170°C.

Add the plain flour, tapioca flour, salt flakes, pepper, oregano, garlic powder, turmeric and curry powder to a large bowl and dry whisk until combined.

Coat half the chicken pieces with a little extra plain flour, dredge in the eggwhite, and finally toss in the seasoned flour. Gently shake off any excess flour and fry for 5 minutes. Drain on paper towel and repeat for the remaining chicken. Refry each batch, starting with the rested chicken first, for 3–4 minutes until cooked – if you have a probe thermometer, the chicken is cooked when the internal temperature reaches 75°C.

For the slaw, add the oil, vinegar and sugar to a large bowl, season and combine. Add the cabbage, corn, onion and half the cheese, season again and toss to coat. Pile onto a serving platter, sprinkle over the remaining cheese and serve with the chicken.

SERVES 4

Fried Brined Chicken with Corn Slaw

This recipe is inspired by David Chang's legendary interpretation of the Korean classic. And, like him, I use roasted pork rather than the more traditional boiled meat. The first time I cooked this was in 2011, or thereabouts, for a good friend's fortieth birthday. It was very experimental back then, but I was just really fascinated by the idea of roasted pork paired with, amongst other things, briny fresh oysters. I have tweaked this feast plenty since then, and added a pile of freshly steamed bao, which were a notable omission from that first attempt. There are no real rules to eating this, except that bo ssam roughly translates to wrapped or enclosed, so take a bao or a lettuce cup and pile in some pork and whichever bits take your fancy.

*In the unlikely event that you have some pork left over, it is great in **Congee** (page 172), or in my **Singapore Noodles** (page 168) instead of duck. And if the thought of making your own kimchi, pickles and bao seems out of reach, you can readily buy them at any Asian grocer.*

150 g brown sugar

150 g sea salt

1 × 2 kg boned pork shoulder (not rolled), skin on

150 ml rice wine vinegar

2 heads butter lettuce, trimmed, leaves separated

1 continental cucumber, finely sliced lengthways

1 bunch of coriander, fine stems and leaves picked

3 limes, cut into wedges

18 Sydney rock oysters, freshly shucked

1 lemon, cut into wedges

1 quantity steamed Bao (page 85)

steamed short grain rice, to serve

250 g Quick Kimchi (page 47)

radish from Spiced Chinese Pickles (page 46), to serve

1 quantity Gochujang Chilli Sauce (page 40)

GINGER & SPRING ONION SAUCE

10 spring onions, white and pale green parts only, finely sliced

10-cm piece of ginger, finely diced

80 ml grapeseed oil (or other neutral oil)

2 tablespoons light soy sauce

2 teaspoons sherry vinegar

1 teaspoon salt flakes

BO SSAM

This recipe will need to be started the day before serving.

Combine the brown sugar and salt in a large ceramic or glass dish. Add the pork and rub thoroughly with the cure. Refrigerate uncovered overnight – you could do this on the day of serving if necessary, but set aside for a minimum of 4 hours.

When ready to cook, preheat the oven to 160°C fan-forced (180°C conventional).

Transfer the pork, skin-side up, to a deep roasting tray, discarding any liquid in the dish but leaving the cure on the meat. Pour over the vinegar, cover with baking paper and foil and roast for 2 hours. Uncover and cook for 1 more hour.

Remove the tray from the oven, lift off the skin and set aside. Baste the meat with the tray juices and place the tray back in the oven for about 1 hour, basting every 20 minutes or so until the meat is just starting to fall apart. Cover the pork loosely with foil and set aside.

Increase the oven to 200°C fan-forced (220°C conventional). Line a baking tray with baking paper.

Flip the skin over and scrape off any fat or meat. Flip back over onto the prepared tray and roast for 15 minutes, turning on the grill for the last 5 minutes – watch carefully, as it can burn quickly. Set aside on the tray to crisp up further – this won't puff up like conventional crackling, but it will still be crisp and crunchy.

For the spring onion sauce, combine all the ingredients in a small bowl and set aside for 10 minutes before using.

To serve, arrange the lettuce, cucumber, coriander and lime wedges on one serving platter, and the oysters and lemon wedges on another. Transfer the pork, crackling and about half the roasting juices to a warm serving dish. Shred some of the meat with tongs, using a knife to loosen if necessary, and turn through the juices. Serve with the freshly steamed bao, rice, kimchi, pickles and gochujang and spring onion sauces on the side.

SERVES 8

Bo Ssam

Until the explosion of interest in real Mexican food, I must admit my experiments were limited to tricking up the supermarket offerings with a bit of spice and coriander. Since then, I've played with the flavours a lot, and though I've ended up including some less than authentic ingredients here alongside the more traditional ones, it's all to build deeper and more intense layers of flavour while still staying true to the spirit.

This became quite a signature weekend feast at our old house. There's a bit of work and planning involved, and I used to always justify the effort by making a lot of food. Before long, the neighbours were drafted in to help us eat it all, with a few always sauntering across just before we had a chance to invite them, especially if I was cooking in the wood-fired oven – the aroma of roasting pork tends to arouse a little neighbourly interest. Some ice-cold beer, a few rounds of margaritas on the rocks in salt-encrusted glasses and the rest of the afternoon or evening would tend to take care of itself.

PULLED PORK BELLY WITH TORTILLAS, LIME & HERB SALSA & CHIPOTLE ADOBO

PULLED PORK BELLY

1 × 2 kg pork belly, bone in
salt flakes and freshly ground
  black pepper
100 ml balsamic vinegar
60 g brown sugar
100 g tamarind paste
80 ml soy sauce
3 heaped tablespoons of Smoky
  Chipotle Adobo (page 42)
1 garlic bulb, skin on, cut in half
  horizontally
1 bunch of coriander, roots only,
  carefully washed
1 onion, skin on, cut in half
2 tablespoons coriander seeds
2 cinnamon sticks

2 teaspoons cloves
2 teaspoons allspice berries
3 bird's eye chillies, split
  lengthways
2 fresh bay leaves
1 fennel bulb, thickly sliced

LIME & HERB SALSA

3 limes, peeled and diced
2 lemons, peeled and diced
3–4 long green chillies,
  deseeded and sliced
10 mint sprigs, leaves picked
  and chopped
1 bunch of coriander, leaves
  picked and finely chopped
10 dill sprigs, fronds picked

5 spring onions, white and pale
  green parts, finely sliced
100 ml extra-virgin olive oil
salt flakes
3 avocados, diced

TO SERVE

20 small corn tortillas
400 g sour cream
pickled jalapeños
¼ red cabbage, shredded
coriander sprigs
lime wedges
Smoky Chipotle Adobo
  (page 42)

This recipe will need to be started the day before serving.

For the pulled pork belly, place the pork belly in a large saucepan, cover with water, add 1 tablespoon of salt flakes and bring to the boil. Reduce the heat to low, simmer for 15 minutes and drain. Score the pork skin while hot and still soft. Wash out the pan and return the pork. Add half the balsamic, half the sugar and the remaining ingredients except for the fennel. Pour in enough water to just cover, and simmer for 1½ hours, topping up with water as required.

Carefully remove the pork from the pan and reserve the cooking liquid. Once cool enough to handle, slip the bones from the meat with your hands and trim away any gristle. Transfer the pork to a tray, skin-side up, and refrigerate overnight, or for about 8 hours – leave the pork uncovered to dry out the skin.

Strain the cooking liquid into a clean saucepan and add the remaining vinegar and sugar. Simmer for about 25 minutes, skimming off any impurities as they appear, until you have a thickened sauce. Refrigerate until needed.

The next day, preheat the oven to 180°C fan-forced (200°C conventional).

Rub the pork all over with salt and pepper and place, skin-side up, on top of the sliced fennel in a roasting tray. Pour in 100 ml of water and 100 ml of the reduced sauce and roast for 35 minutes. Turn the heat up to 200°C fan-forced (220°C conventional), uncover and roast for a further 15 minutes to crisp up the skin – keep an eye on it, you want it quite dark but don't let it burn.

Meanwhile, reheat the reduced sauce.

For the salsa, combine all the ingredients except the avocado in a medium bowl. Season and set aside for 5 minutes. Place the avocado in a serving bowl and pour over the salsa.

When you are almost ready to serve, wrap the tortillas in baking paper and foil and warm in the oven for a few minutes.

Slice the pork, shred with a fork and coat with the reduced sauce. Serve with the sour cream, jalapeños, cabbage, coriander, lime, adobo sauce and tortillas on the side.

SERVES 6–8

Pulled Pork Belly with Tortillas, Lime & Herb Salsa & Chipotle Adobo

Bistecca alla Fiorentina – the name is a tribute to the legendary Chianina steak of Florence – was a cornerstone of my old restaurant, the Melbourne Wine Room. For fifteen-odd years it was never off the menu. With the luxury of a real chargrill – unlike the gas versions that so many restaurants use – we were able to do the meat justice with a thick crust and genuine smoky char. The great thing is you can easily replicate the method at home, as long as you take the time to build a good, even bed of coals.

There are no better accompaniments to the deep flavour of the charred meat than some great oil and Dijon, a good squeeze of lemon and this peppery horseradish mix. Be sure to choose a large dry-aged steak from a mature, grass-fed animal.

BISTECCA ALLA FIORENTINA

2 × 600–700 g dry-aged grass-fed rib eye steaks

olive oil, for grilling

100 g Sicilian sea salt or fine Himalayan salt

30 g freshly ground white pepper

premium extra-virgin olive oil, to serve

lemons wedges, to serve

mustard, to serve

HORSERADISH MIX

1 small celeriac, peeled

1 fresh horseradish root, peeled (or 100 g unsweetened prepared horseradish)

1 tablespoon Dijon mustard

1 tablespoon extra-virgin olive oil

salt flakes and freshly ground black pepper

½ lemon

Light the barbecue using wood or charcoal as fuel.

Take the steaks from the fridge at least 1 hour before cooking to bring them up to room temperature – this will ensure more even and accurate cooking.

For the horseradish mix, finely grate the celeriac into a sieve. Gently squeeze out any excess liquid and add to a medium bowl. Finely grate the horseradish into the bowl, then add the Dijon and oil and mix to combine. Season and squeeze in lemon juice to taste – you can make this at any point, but it will need to sit for at least 15 minutes before using.

Once the flames have subsided and the coals are peaking in temperature, allow them to settle for about 30 minutes until you have an even heat.

Place the steaks on a tray and lightly coat them all over with the olive oil. Combine the salt and white pepper in a small bowl and pack generously onto each side of each steak – this may seem like a lot, but some will be lost on the grill and it will help to protect the meat and fat from burning.

Place the steaks on the hottest part of the grill. If the coals flame, move the steaks to where they don't – if you burn the fat you will ruin the flavour of the steak. Seal the steaks for 4 minutes on one side, turn over and cook for 3 minutes. Remove from the grill and rest for 6 minutes somewhere warm.

Place the steaks back on the grill and cook for 3 minutes on each side for medium–rare. You only need to rest the steaks for a minute or so at this stage, as they have been rested after the primary cooking.

Serve as is, or slice off the bone and cut into four. Drizzle lavishly with extra-virgin olive oil and serve with lemon wedges, a dollop of mustard and horseradish mix on the side.

SERVES 2–4

DRY-AGED BEEF

My meat supplier of choice is fourth generation butcher Gary McBean, who specialises in grass-fed, dry-aged beef, as well as rare-breed pork and saltbush lamb. Gary started helping in his father's shop when he was only nine or ten and was officially taken on as an apprentice when he was fourteen. Back then, things were done much the same way that he does them now, the beef came from mature animals around two and a half to three years old and it was carefully dry-aged to improve the flavour and texture.

But it hasn't always been like that, in the intervening years when fat was public enemy number one, he couldn't sell a steak that wasn't lean. As a consequence, all meat needed to come from younger animals that hadn't developed much intramuscular fat, and then it needed to be trimmed as leanly as possible. You can't age beef without a good layer of fat and the beasts that have this tend to be mature and have developed good marbling and an intense beefy flavour.

A time-honoured practice was sadly fading, and although Gary still kept ageing beef the way his father, grandfather and great-grandfather had before him, it was very much a backroom affair with a small, though very loyal, customer base. Thankfully, attitudes have changed, and a few years back Gary took a punt on making his ageing room a shop-length glass cabinet, and he hasn't looked back since.

Dry-ageing beef at a low temperature enables enzymes already present in the meat to, over time, break down muscle fibres and tenderise the meat. During the ageing process the fat also experiences oxidative changes and develops its distinctive dry-aged flavour – admittedly not for everyone. There is some water loss in the ageing process, but this is relatively minimal once the outside of the meat has developed a crust, meaning that a steak aged for thirty or sixty days – or even double this in some of Gary's experiments – is still moist and succulent and actually retains most of this during the cooking process, unlike a fresh or wet-aged steak.

The difference in the quality of meat from an animal that has been reared slowly to maturity on pasture alone, and then dry-aged in ideal conditions just can't be compared to a young animal fattened rapidly on grain, butchered and sold immediately. Yes, it's more expensive, but meat like this should be cherished and respected, and its intensity and richness is really quite satisfying.

Bistecca alla Fiorentina

SWEET STUFF

A LITTLE SOMETHING TO FINISH

———

COCONUT MARSHMALLOW KISSES

LEMON & POPPY SEED BISCUITS

**ROASTED PEARS WITH GORGONZOLA,
TOASTED WALNUTS, WATERCRESS & ROCKET**

**TAMARILLOS POACHED IN ROSÉ,
VANILLA & ROSE GERANIUM**

**LIME & COCONUT TART
WITH MARSHMALLOW KISSES**

**CUCUMBER & LIME GRANITA, GIN JELLY,
YOGHURT SORBET & MINTED CUCUMBER**

LEMON CREAM & CHERRY POSSETS

SLOW-BAKED APPLE PIE

———

*These airy, coconut-scented marshmallows are pretty delicious on their own, but they also add a nice touch to my **Lime & Coconut Tart** (page 254), or try making your own snowballs by shaping the mix into small domes and dipping them in chocolate and desiccated coconut. For a more substantial treat, smooth the marshmallow into a lined brownie tray dusted with the icing sugar mix. Once set, slice with a hot knife into cubes or slabs, roll in coconut and dust with more of the icing sugar mix. Whichever shape you decide on, wrapped nicely these make great little gifts.*

COCONUT MARSHMALLOW KISSES

12 g gold-strength leaf gelatine
70 g pure icing sugar
70 g cornflour
200 g caster sugar
20 g liquid glucose
80 g eggwhites (about 4 eggs)
1 teaspoon natural coconut essence
½ cup shredded coconut

You will need a candy thermometer for this recipe.

Line two baking trays with baking paper.

Add the gelatine to a small jug or bowl of cold water and set aside for about 5 minutes.

Combine the icing sugar and cornflour in a sifter or fine sieve and set aside.

Add the caster sugar, glucose and 1½ tablespoons of water to a medium saucepan and heat to 121°C.

Meanwhile, add the eggwhites to the bowl of a stand mixer and whisk on medium to stiff peaks.

Once the sugar reaches temperature, take the pan off the heat and add the gelatine, squeezed of any excess water, and stir to dissolve. Reduce the speed of the mixer and slowly pour the hot syrup down the side of the bowl. Once incorporated, add the coconut essence and increase the speed to high. Whisk until the mix is cool, glossy and quite stiff, about 10 minutes. Scoop the marshmallow into a piping bag fitted with a small plain nozzle.

Sift a light dusting of the icing sugar mix over the prepared trays. Pipe the marshmallow on as desired, sprinkle over the shredded coconut and dust with more of the icing sugar mix. Set aside at room temperature for 1 hour to set. Store in an airtight container.

MAKES ABOUT 50

These deliciously short and buttery biscuits have a real lemony tang to them that I just love. They are perfect to have on hand to enjoy with a cup of tea, or they can be crushed up and sprinkled over a panna cotta or a scoop of ice cream.

LEMON & POPPY SEED BISCUITS

125 ml lemon juice (about 3 lemons)

250 g unsalted butter

420 g plain flour

1 teaspoon baking powder

½ teaspoon salt flakes

200 g caster sugar

2 tablespoons honey

1 extra-large egg

1 teaspoon vanilla extract

1 tablespoon finely grated lemon zest, plus ½ teaspoon extra to serve

2 tablespoons poppy seeds

Preheat the oven to 170°C fan-forced (190°C conventional). Line two baking trays with baking paper.

Bring the lemon juice to a simmer in a small saucepan and reduce by half. Add 100 g of butter and whisk until melted. Remove from the heat and set aside.

Combine the flour, baking powder and salt in a large bowl and dry whisk to break up any clumps.

Add the remaining butter, 150 g of sugar and the honey to the bowl of a stand mixer and whisk until pale and fluffy. Add the egg and lemon juice and butter mix and beat on medium–high for about 3 minutes until very light and pale. Mix in the vanilla, 1 tablespoon of lemon zest and 1 tablespoon of poppy seeds. Once combined, reduce the speed to low, add the dry mix and beat until smooth. Cover the bowl and refrigerate for 20 minutes.

Roll walnut-sized balls of the rested dough and place on the prepared trays, leaving at least 4 cm between each to allow for spreading.

Combine the remaining sugar with ½ teaspoon of lemon zest. Using a slightly moist glass, dip the base into the sugar and zest mix and use it to flatten one of the balls slightly. Repeat for all the cookies, dipping the glass in the sugar mix each time. Sprinkle the remaining poppy seeds over the cookies and bake for about 15 minutes until lightly golden around the edges. Cool for a few minutes on the trays before cooling completely on wire racks.

MAKES ABOUT 28

The pears take up the subtle hint of thyme and the gentle sweetness and acid from the verjuice as they roast, making them an ideal foil for the salty and pungent Gorgonzola. This can be served as a cheese course, or also works well as a little entree or antipasti course. If blue cheese is a bit strong for your taste, try this with some Parmigiano–Reggiano or aged ashed chevre instead.

ROASTED PEARS WITH GORGONZOLA, TOASTED WALNUTS, WATERCRESS & ROCKET

5 Corella pears, thickly sliced lengthways and tossed in the juice of ½ lemon

1 ½ tablespoons brown sugar

100 ml verjuice

1 ½ tablespoons extra-virgin olive oil

freshly ground black pepper

4 thyme sprigs

6 thin slices of sourdough rye bread

150 g Gorgonzola Piccante

80 g walnuts, toasted and tossed in extra-virgin olive oil and salt flakes while warm

2 handfuls of mixed mustard cress, rocket and watercress

1 tablespoon fennel fronds (optional)

Preheat the oven to 180°C fan-forced (200°C conventional).

Add the pears to a medium roasting tray and sprinkle over the sugar, verjuice and oil. Grind over a good amount of pepper and scatter over the thyme. Roast for about 30 minutes until the pears are tender and slightly golden. Set aside to cool.

Toast the bread.

Arrange the pears on a platter. Shave the Gorgonzola and scatter over the pears, followed by the walnuts, greens and fennel fronds (if using). Drizzle over some of the roasting juices and serve with the rye toast.

SERVES 4

VERJUICE

Verjuice or verjus is simply the juice of unripe grapes, and sometimes other fruits. It's tartly sweet but much milder in acidity than lemon juice and doesn't have the sharp tang of vinegar. We all owe a debt to Maggie Beer for being able to use verjuice at all, unless, of course, you happen to live on a vineyard. Maggie hasn't only broadened our knowledge of its uses, but she actually made it commercially available for the first time. Use it to add sweetness and a balancing spike of gentle acidity to salad dressings and sauces, to deglaze a pan, to enrich and also to refresh fish, chicken or pork dishes. Verjuice will deteriorate and oxidise once opened, so only buy what you need.

*Tamarillos have such a beautifully distinctive flavour that is enhanced by poaching them in syrup, which also helps to balance out their intensely sour profile. The rose geranium leaves add such amazing fragrance to the poaching liquid, but if you can't locate them, just add a splash of rosewater to the syrup once the tamarillos are cooked. You can order rose geranium leaves from a specialist grocer, but it's easier to buy a plant at a nursery so that you'll always have the beautifully aromatic leaves on hand to flavour syrups and jams (try my **Simple Roasted Raspberry Jam** on page 14).*

TAMARILLOS POACHED IN ROSÉ, VANILLA & ROSE GERANIUM

10 red tamarillos

750 ml rosé wine

450 g caster sugar

1 vanilla bean, sliced on an angle

2 handfuls of rose geranium leaves

cream, ice cream or natural yoghurt, to serve

Score a cross in the skin at the tip of each tamarillo and blanch in boiling water for 2 minutes. Plunge into iced water and peel, leaving the stems intact if possible. Reserve the skins – this is where the colour comes from.

Add the wine, sugar, vanilla, geranium leaves and tamarillo skins to a large saucepan and bring to the boil. Turn down the heat, stir to dissolve the sugar and simmer for 2 minutes. Remove the skins and reduce the heat. Add the tamarillos to the liquid, cover with a cartouche made out of baking paper and poach over low heat for about 20 minutes until tender.

Once cooked, cool the tamarillos completely in the syrup. Serve with a drizzle of the poaching syrup and cream, ice cream or yoghurt.

SERVES 10

Lemon tarts seemed invincible in the nineties, an almost immovable fixture on so many restaurant lists. And while they may have fallen a little out of fashion, no tweaking or reinventing can improve on such a beautifully simple classic. However, I'm currently a bit more partial to the exotic scents of lime and coconut in this close relative – and not just because the flavours are just that little more of the moment.

The coconut adds a chewy and resilient yet deliciously crumbly texture to this pastry, as well as echoing the flavour of the filling. You could leave the marshmallows off, but I do really like the airy textural contrast with the luscious, tangy curd, crumbly pastry and fresh cream.

LIME & COCONUT TART WITH MARSHMALLOW KISSES

300 ml cream (35% fat), stiffly whipped
20–25 Coconut Marshmallow Kisses (page 246)
finely grated zest of 1 lime
1 handful of shredded coconut

PASTRY
200 g plain flour
100 g desiccated coconut
100 g pure icing sugar
1 pinch of salt flakes
125 g unsalted butter, diced
1 extra-large egg
2 extra-large egg yolks

TART FILLING
300 g caster sugar
finely grated zest and juice of 4 limes and 2 lemons (250–300 ml juice in total)
4 eggs
2 egg yolks
200 ml thick coconut cream
80 ml cream (35% fat)

Preheat the oven to 180°C fan-forced (200°C conventional).

For the pastry, pulse the flour, desiccated coconut, icing sugar, salt and butter in a food processor until a coarse crumb forms. Add the egg and egg yolks and pulse again to bring the pastry together. Tip onto a bench and form into a ball, wrap in plastic wrap and refrigerate for 30 minutes.

Remove the pastry from the fridge and roll out between two pieces of lightly floured baking paper until 5 mm thick. Remove the baking paper and carefully roll up on the rolling pin. Unroll over a 28-cm loose-bottomed flan tin and press the pastry into the tin, taking care to press evenly into the fluted edges. Refrigerate for 10 minutes.

Place the tart tin on a baking tray and line the inside of the shell with foil or baking paper. Fill with pastry weights, rice or dried beans and bake for 15 minutes. Remove the foil and weights and cook for another 5 minutes until golden. Set aside to cool.

Reduce the oven to 160°C fan-forced (180°C conventional).

For the filling, blitz the sugar and lime and lemon zest in a food processor. Add the lime and lemon juice and blitz to combine.

Add the eggs, egg yolks, coconut cream and cream to the bowl of a stand mixer and beat until combined. Add the sugar and citrus mix and beat until combined. Pour the filling into the tart shell and bake for 30–40 minutes until just set. Set aside to cool.

Fit a piping bag with a fine nozzle and fill with the whipped cream. Pipe dollops of cream all over the cooled tart, arrange the marshmallow kisses on top, scatter over the lime zest and shredded coconut and serve.

SERVES 6

This is my kind of dessert: refreshing and bright with the sweetness balanced out by citric acidity and a spicy punch from the gin jelly. This is enough of a dessert course for me, but you could also treat this as a little refresher course to show off after main course and before you get into anything seriously sweet and rich. I like to use Yarra Valley's own Four Pillars Gin for this (amongst other things), as it's intensely spicy with plenty of citrus and Australian botanicals.

CUCUMBER & LIME GRANITA, GIN JELLY, YOGHURT SORBET & MINTED CUCUMBER

150 g caster sugar

1 continental cucumber

1 handful of mint leaves, finely shredded

500 ml yoghurt sorbet

GRANITA

3 continental cucumbers

100 g caster sugar, plus 1½ tablespoons extra

100 ml lime juice (about 4 limes)

finely grated zest of 2 limes

GIN JELLY

8 leaves of gold-strength gelatine

300 ml quality aromatic gin (such as Four Pillars, Martin Miller's or Hendrick's)

For the granita, grate the cucumbers, skin and all, into a large bowl. Sprinkle over 1½ tablespoons of sugar and set aside for 10 minutes. Strain through a fine sieve into a medium bowl and discard the solids.

Gently warm the lime juice, lime zest and 100 g of sugar in a small saucepan, stirring until the sugar has dissolved – don't get this too warm or you will change the flavour of the cucumber juice once combined. Tip into the bowl with the cucumber juice and stir to combine. Pour the mix into a shallow glass or plastic dish, cover and freeze for 5–6 hours, or overnight.

For the gin jelly, add the gelatine to a small jug or bowl of cold water and set aside for about 5 minutes. Gently warm 200 ml of water in a small saucepan and take off the heat. Add the gelatine, squeezed of excess water, and stir to dissolve. Add the gin and stir to combine. Pour into eight glasses and refrigerate until set, about 3 hours.

Add the caster sugar and 100 ml of water to a small saucepan and bring to the boil. Stir until the sugar has dissolved. Refrigerate until cold and syrupy.

Using a small Parisian baller, scoop out balls of cucumber and add to a medium bowl. Add the mint and enough syrup to coat. Toss gently and add to the glasses along with small scoops of sorbet. Scratch the surface of the granita with a fork until fluffy and drop into the glasses. Serve immediately.

SERVES 8

This is quite an elegant and sophisticated little dessert, perfect for more formal entertaining, but just as suited to a casual stand-up affair. These would make ideal little desserts at Christmas when cherries are at their best. The possets can be made well ahead of time and garnished and presented in a flash, leaving the hard work well behind you and, hopefully, the dishes to someone else.

LEMON CREAM & CHERRY POSSETS

600 g cherries
80 g raw sugar
50 g raspberry jam
½ teaspoon vanilla bean paste
juice of ½ lemon

LEMON CREAM
finely grated zest and juice of
  2 lemons (about 120 ml juice)
150 g raw sugar
500 ml double cream
200 ml cream (35% fat)

Set ten of the best looking cherries with stalks aside to decorate each posset. Pit the remaining cherries and cut them in half. Add to a large bowl with the sugar and toss to combine. Add half the cherries and sugar to a medium saucepan and set the remainder aside for 1 hour to macerate.

Add the jam, vanilla bean paste and lemon juice to the pan with the cherries and cook over medium heat for 5 minutes until softened.

Tip the cooked cherry mix into a blender and puree until smooth. Pass through a fine sieve and divide between ten serving glasses. Once macerated, divide the remaining cherries between the glasses and refrigerate.

For the lemon cream, add the lemon zest and sugar to a food processor and blitz until well combined. Add the zest and sugar mix, double cream and cream to a medium saucepan and bring to a gentle simmer. Once the sugar has dissolved, take off the heat and add the lemon juice. Strain immediately and divide between the glasses. Chill for 3–4 hours until set.

Garnish each posset with a reserved cherry and serve.

SERVES 10

CHERRIES

Cherries pop up in the markets at all times of the year, sourced from various international harvests, but I like to stick to the local ones and properly celebrate their relatively brief but beautiful season. In late spring and early summer, I tend to enjoy them just as they are, and a box or two is a Christmas necessity in our house – they're beautiful served on ice if Christmas Day is a hot one. When they're at their cheapest and most abundant or when the season is tailing off, I'll get out my big copper jam pan so that I can hoard some of the harvest for the coming cherry-less months.

The aroma of clove-studded apple pie brings back such vivid childhood memories for me, and even if the pastry was sometimes a little on the soggy side, it was still always delicious. This is a genuine old-fashioned pie, slow-cooked and with a full pastry crust. A real pie, none of that pastry lid on a pie dish stuff! Try making this with new-season organic apples, not only are they so much tastier than the ones that have been sitting in a cool store for months, they'll be just as cheap and the weather around harvest time will be perfect for a warming apple pie.

SLOW-BAKED APPLE PIE

180 g golden caster sugar
juice of 1 lemon
1 ½ tablespoons cornflour
5 cloves
1.5 kg small apples, cored, peeled and sliced (900 g prepared weight)
500 g puff pastry
1 tablespoon cream (35% fat)
cream or custard, to serve

Preheat the oven to 180°C fan-forced (200°C conventional). Grease a 24-cm springform cake tin. Line a baking tray with baking paper.

Combine 160 g of sugar, the lemon juice, cornflour and cloves in a large bowl. Add the apples and toss to coat.

Roll two-thirds of the pastry out until just under 1 cm thick. Carefully line the prepared tin with the pastry, allowing the pastry to hang over the rim of the tin. Tip in the apples and gently flatten them.

Roll out the remaining pastry into a circle about 1 cm thick. Brush the edge with a little cream and place on top of the apple mix with the brushed edge facing down. Press the edges together and trim so that about 2 cm of the pastry overhangs the lip. Loosely fold the overhang back into the tin and brush all the exposed pastry with a little more cream. Sprinkle over the remaining sugar and make a few incisions in the pastry for the steam to escape. Place the tin on the prepared tray and bake for 30 minutes.

Reduce the temperature to 150°C fan-forced (170°C conventional) and cook for a further 40 minutes until the crust is golden and the apples are bubbling beneath the pastry. Cool for 25 minutes for the filling to set. Serve with cream or custard.

SERVES 8

ACKNOWLEDGEMENTS

Thank you to my dear family and friends for your kind words, encouragement, patience and never-ending appetite for pretty much anything I dish up. You know who you are. I love and appreciate you all dearly.

Very special love and appreciation to my sister Odette for all of the recipe advice and for tweaking everything so perfectly. You are very talented, very particular and very precise – thank you Odie.

Special mention to Emma King for lending a knowledgeable and kind ear, day or night. I treasure our free-flow chats, as well as your great cooking and attitude to food.

To Marcus Ellis, for your patience, diligence, sense of humour and attention to detail during this entire project – I couldn't have done it without you. You have enriched this book endlessly with your knowledge and word-smithing. I know it's going to be a great success, so thank you and here's to many more in the future.

To the talented Chantal Faux – thanks for managing, creating and fielding so many of my personal enquiries. I treasure our friendship and am lucky to have had your keen ear since the very humble beginnings of the KM brand.

To Mary Small and Jane Winning – thanks again for your endless enthusiasm. What a quick turnaround and what a marvellous outcome! Thanks also to the whole team at Pan Macmillan for channelling a fresh vision and energy into this book. I have enjoyed every minute of getting to know you and truly appreciate and admire your expertise in the increasingly competitive world of publishing.

Thank you to talented designer Kirby Armstrong for creating such a beautiful, simple and confident layout for the book. I am so happy with it.

Thanks to proofreader Megan Johnston, typesetter Pauline Haas and indexer Jo Rudd for their editorial attention and eye for detail.

Extra love and a super-big hug to Emma Warren Rodriguez. As always, it was a job perfectly done. I really appreciate your attention to every detail and your ability to make everyone feel at ease. You have been around to help at every stage of the process, from the endless chats in the beginning all the way through to the finish line. It was a massive coordination job done extremely well, with lots of laughs along the way.

Thank you Paris for your contribution to the concept stage of this book – your opinion is truly valued. You are fabulous and a real jack-of-all-trades. Thanks for tying up all the loose ends and coordinating this crazy life I lead with a constant smile, no matter what the request (and for managing to be in another country during the entire shoot!).

Thanks to Julie Provis for the beautiful make-up on the cover shoot.

Special thanks to all the chefs and other people who helped, both on set and behind the scenes – my head chef Sushil Rana,

Badal, and also to Meryl Batlle for assisting on the shoot. This is a massive achievement and I really appreciate your attention to detail.

To my wonderful, knowledgeable suppliers who always go the extra distance to supply the best and the freshest: Gary McBean at Gary's Quality Meats at Prahran Market; Sam and John Narduzzo, Mark and the whole team at Pino's Fine Produce; Prahran Seafood; Claringbold's Seafood; Pete 'n' Rosie's Deli; Ripe Organics; and Damian Pike.

Thank you to stylist Deborah Kaloper. I appreciate your styling knowledge, expertise and perfect artistic eye. It was a pleasure working with you, and I believe we have made a very special book.

To photographer Mark Chew, I love your work. It's so wonderful to have you see my food as I do and then capture it in the most beautiful images. You were truly a delight to work with – let's do it again.

A big thanks to Cathy Baker at CMC Talent for your trusted opinion on all of my crazy ideas (which you bring to life whenever possible) and for your effortless negotiation along the way.

Finally, to my partner, Michael, and our girls, Stella and Amber, thank you. Mike, you keep me grounded, focused, inspired and supported, doing all of this rather effortlessly, laughing all the way and making so much happen behind the scenes. Stella and Amber, from the bottom of my heart, you two are my inspiration and my little treasures. You are always happy to taste and contribute your valuable and amusing opinions on pretty much anything I cook. This book wouldn't be so special without all of you.

Karen x

INDEX

A PLUM BOOK

First published in 2015 by
Pan Macmillan Australia Pty Limited
Level 25, 1 Market Street,
Sydney, NSW 2000, Australia

Level 1, 15–19 Claremont Street,
South Yarra, Victoria 3141, Australia

Design by Kirby Armstrong
Photography by Mark Chew
Styling by Deborah Kaloper
Edited by Marcus Ellis
Typeset by Pauline Haas
Index by Jo Rudd
Colour reproduction by Splitting Image Colour Studio
Printed and bound in China by 1010 Printing International Limited

A CIP catalogue record for this book is available from the National Library of
Australia.

The publisher would like to thank the following for their generosity in providing
props for the book: Hale Mercantile Co. Linen Merchants, Hamish & Grace,
Marimekko, Safari Living and Sarah Schembri Ceramics.

10 9 8 7 6 5 4 3 2 1